THE

ENGLISHWOMAN IN EGYPT:

LETTERS FROM CAIRO,

WRITTEN DURING A RESIDENCE THERE IN 1842, 3, & 4,

WITH

E. W. LANE, Esq.

AUTHOR OF 'THE MODERN EGYPTIANS.'

BY HIS SISTER.

IN TWO VOLUMES—VOL. II.

British Library Cataloguing-in-Publication Data
A catalogue record for this book is available from the
British Library

CONTENTS.

LETTER XXIV.

LETTER XXV.

LETTER XXVI.

LETTER XXVII.

LETTER XXVIII.

THE

ENGLISHWOMAN IN EGYPT.

LETTER XVII.

April, 1843.

MY DEAR FRIEND,

You will congratulate us on our having quitted " the haunted house ;" and you will do so heartily when I tell you that six families have succeeded each other in it, in as many weeks, since our departure. The sixth family was about to quit immediately when we heard this news ; five having been driven out by most obstinate persecutions, not only during the nights, but in broad daylight, of so violent a description, that the windows were all broken in a large upper chamber, our favourite room. The sixth family suffered similar annoyances, and also complained that much of their china was demolished. Like ourselves, no one has been able to obtain quiet rest in that house,

B

or rather I should say, others have been in a worse
state than ourselves, for we obtained some relief
in consequence of our doorkeeper's achievement.
And now I hope I have done with this subject.   I
have said much upon it, but I must be held ex-
cusable, as "'tis passing strange."

Our present house is extremely commodious, and
much taste and judgment have been displayed in its
construction.   The terrace is extensive and very
picturesque, and the upper rooms are well situated.
Most of the rooms are furnished with glass windows, and the house altogether, being exceedingly
well built, is adapted for affording warmth in the
winter, and proving a cool summer residence.

With regard to a sojourn in Egypt, it is not an
easy matter to give you the *pour et contre*.   Of
one thing I am convinced, that persons must remain a year in this country, that is, they must go
the round of the seasons, or nearly so, before they
can fully judge of the comforts it offers.   I well
remember the extreme annoyance I experienced,
for some months after our arrival, from the unusually prolonged heat, of which I complained to
you, and from the flies and musquitoes, which were
really and constantly distressing; and I could
scarcely believe what people told me, namely, that
I should soon find myself very well contented with
the climate of the country.   As to the musquitoes,
they interfere so much with enjoyment, that a tra-

veller who visits Egypt only during the great heat
may assert, with truth, that he has no comfort by
day, nor by night until he enters his curtain. I
confess that I often feared we could not remain
here as long as I wished. No sooner, however,
did the Nile subside, than my hopes revived ; and
finding that the most charming temperature imaginable succeeded the heat, I began to understand
what travellers mean when they call this a delicious
climate.   November is a sweet month here—December and January are rather too cold, taking
into consideration that there are neither fire-places
nor chimneys in any of the houses, excepting in
the kitchens.   February and March are perfectly
delightful, the temperature then being almost as
mild as that of summer in England.   During
April there occur some instances of hot wind,
otherwise it is an agreeable month.   In May the
hot winds are trying, and then follow four months
of oppressive heat.

Devoted as I am, justly, to my own dear country
and her blessed associations, I can give you my
candid opinion, without any fear that I shall be suspected of preferring a residence in the Levant to my
English home, and will show you, without reserve,
in what consist the fascinations of this part of the
East ;—in the climate, in the manners of the
people, and in the simplicity of their habits, which
not only attract my admiration, but render me
2

much less affected by their general poverty than I am by less distress in my own country. It is very certain that if a daily journal were published in Cairo, we should not see paragraphs headed " death by starvation," " distressing case," &c.; but why is it? for there are no houses here for the reception of the poor, as in England. It results from the contented spirit of the poor, if provided simply with bread and water; and, more than all, from the sort of family union which subsists throughout the East, and which literally teaches the poor to " bear each other's burthens." In visiting the middle and higher classes of society, the same family compact is observable, and the mother of the family continues always the mother and the head; her gentle reign lasting with her valued life, and the love and respect of those around her increasing with her years. It is asserted, that when Mohammed was asked what relation had the strongest claim on affection and respect, he replied with warmth, " The mother! the mother! the mother!"

All blood relations in the East take precedence of the wife, who is received into a family as a younger sister. It could scarcely be suffered here, or in Turkey, that a father or mother should quit a house to make way for a son's wife. This you will remember is remarked in Mr. Urquhart's ' Spirit of the East;' and let me ask you, is not this as it should be? I cannot understand how any person with a spark of nature in his breast could allow a beloved parent to resign what a child should be willing to shed his heart's blood to preserve.

In obtaining an insight into the habits and manners of the women, I possess considerable advantages; first, from my brother's knowledge of the East, and secondly, from my plan of adhering strictly to habits cherished by the people, which system has secured at once their respect, while it has excited their surprise. We have even gone so far as to adopt their manner of eating; and here I must digress to beg you not to say " How very disgusting !" but read *how* we do it, and then you may confess that it is not so unpleasant as you thought. The dishes are prepared in a very delicate manner ; for instance, small cucumbers and other vegetables of a similar kind are scooped out and stuffed with minced meat and rice ; minced meat is wrapped in vine-leaves, and so dexterously cooked, that each leaf with its contents continues compact, and is easily taken in the fingers. Fried meat in cakes, and the same in form of sausages, are equally convenient ; and all I have mentioned, and a hundred others (for there is great variety in their cookery), may be taken almost as delicately as a slice of cake. For soups, rice prepared in the Eastern manner, and stews, we use spoons ; and so do the Turks. One difficulty occasionally

presents itself; but not at home. The chief lady
of a house, to do her guests honour, presents them
with morsels of her own selection, with her own
fingers; and in some cases repeats this compliment
frequently. It would be a positive affront to
refuse these; and I am quite sure that no Englishwoman can so far strain her politeness as to eat as
much as her hostess, in her excessive hospitality,
desires, though the latter sets her a wonderful example. I have really seen the ladies of this country eat as much as should suffice for three or four
moderate meals at one sitting. But to return to
my difficulty. I always found it to be the best
plan to receive readily, for a time, the morsels
which were offered; and when satisfied, to accept
perhaps another, and sometimes two or three; at
the same time assuring my entertainer, that they
were redundant, but that her viands were so extremely well chosen, that I must, after the repast,
inquire who has superintended the *cuisine*, and
derive from her some information. Thus I removed the impression which was immediately
formed, that the dinner was not dressed agreeably
with my taste: and induced only the remark, that
" the English eat so much less than the Easterns;"
accompanied by regret that so little satisfied me,
but followed by an expression of pleasure that the
dinner was so agreeable to me.

I have not found the system of Eastern etiquette

difficult of adoption; and from the honourable
manner in which I have been received, and treated,
and always pressed to repeat my visit, I may draw
the conclusion fairly, that I have understood how
to please the people. It has been a favourite
opinion of mine, and one in which I have been
educated, that a little quiet observation of the
manners and habits of others will always prevent
those differences about trifles which so often dis-
turb society, and sometimes separate even friends.
Here I have indeed found the advantage of exer-
cising this observation, and it has proved the means
of securing to me invariably polite attention and
respect.

I think you would be amused could you see our
dinner-arrangements at home. First, a small carpet is spread on the mat; then, a stool cased with
mother-of-pearl, &c. is placed upon it, and serves as
the support of a round tray of tinned copper, on
which is arranged our dinner, with a cake of bread
for each person. A maid then brings a copper
ewer and basin, and pours water on the hands
of each of our party, and we arrange ourselves
round the tray, our Eastern table-napkins spread
on our knees. These are larger and longer than
English hand-towels, that they may cover both knees
when sitting in the Turkish manner. During the
meal, the maid holds a water-bottle, or defends us
from flies with a fly-whisk. Having no change of

plates, knives, or forks, no time is lost at dinner; and it usually occupies twenty minutes. Thus, much valuable time is saved by avoiding works of supererogation. One or two sweet dishes are placed on the tray with those which are savoury; and it is singular to see the women of this country take morsels of sweet and savoury food almost alternately. Immediately after dinner, the ewer and basin are brought round, the stool and carpet are removed with the tray, and the stool is always placed in another room until again required. There is something very sociable in this mode of sitting at table, and it is surprising to see how many persons can sit with comfort round a comparatively small tray. I should advise you and other friends in England to resume the use of small round tables: I have often regretted they are no longer in fashion: for a small family, they are infinitely more comfortable than the large square or oblong tables used in England.

It is true, as you suppose, that I am sometimes amused at my position, and more particularly so, when, on the occasion of any thing heavy being brought into the hareem, one of the men passes through the passage belonging to it. Their approach is always announced by their saying audibly, " O Protector! (Ya Sátir) and " Permission!" (Destoor), several times. Excepting on such occasions, no man approaches the hareem but the sakka, or water-carrier; and I often think that any person with a knowledge of Arabic, and none of the habits of the people, would think these sakkas devotees, judging by their constant religious ejaculations. The men are quite as careful in avoiding the hareem, as the ladies are in concealing their faces, and indeed, in many cases, more so. I have been amused particularly by the care of one of our men, who, having lived many years in a Turkish family, is quite a Turkish servant. On one occasion, on returning home from riding with my boys, my donkey fairly threw me off as he entered the court; and when this man raised me up (for my head was on the ground), I supported myself for a moment with my hands against the wall of the house, while I assured my poor children, who were exceedingly frightened, that I was not hurt, forgetting that I was *showing my hands* not only to our own men, but to the men who attended the donkeys! I was immediately recalled to a consciousness of where I was, and of the impropriety of such an exposure, by the servant I have mentioned, who most respectfully covered my hands with my habarah, and wrapped it around me so scrupulously that the men had not a second time the advantage of seeing a finger.

No person can imagine the strictness of the hareem without adopting its seclusion, nor can a stranger form a just estimate of the degree of liberty enjoyed by the women without mixing in Eastern society. One thing is certain, that if a husband be a tyrant, his wife is his slave; but such cases are extremely rare. I do not pretend to defend the system of marrying blindfold, as it were; nor do I look for those happy marriages which are most frequently found in England; but I am pleased to find the Eastern women contented, and, without a single exception among my acquaintances, so cheerful, that I naturally conclude they are treated with consideration. The middle classes are at liberty to pay visits, and to go to the bath, when they please; but their fathers and husbands object to their shopping; therefore female brokers are in the frequent habit of attending the hareems. The higher orders are more closely guarded, yet as this very circumstance is a mark of distinction, the women congratulate each other on this subject; and it is not uncommon for a husband to give his wife a pet name, expressive of her hidden charms, such as " the concealed jewel."

There lives opposite to us a good old woman, a devotee, who is a sort of Deborah to the quarter, and who passes judgment from her projecting window on all cases which are proposed for her opinion, much to our edification. One occurred a few days since, which will show you that the system I have described is not confined to any particular grade in society. A young man in the neighbourhood had

been betrothed to a very young girl, upon the re-
commendation of his fellow-servant, without sending any of his own female relations to ascertain if
her appearance were agreeable, or the reverse.
Becoming anxious on this subject, two days after
the betrothal, he sent a female friend, who asserted
that his bride had but one eye, that she was pitiable
in appearance, and unfit to become his wife. The
person who had recommended her was a married
man, and the bridegroom accused him of culpable
negligence, in not having ascertained whether she
had two eyes or not, as he might have sent his wife
to pay her a visit; while, on his own part, he had
taken no such precaution, and, being the most
interested, was certainly the most to blame. Such
was the state of the case when referred to Deborah.
After hearing it patiently, she said to the young
man, " My son, why did you consent to be betrothed to a girl who was not known to your
mother and to the women of your house?" " They
have been, since my betrothal, to see her," he answered, in a very melancholy tone of voice, " but
she sat in a dark room, and they could not tell
whether she had two eyes or not; and, in truth, O
my mother, I have bought her many articles of
dress, and I have paid four hundred piastres as her
dowry, the savings of many months." " Has she
learnt any trade," asked the old woman, " that so
much was required as her dowry?" " No," re-

plied the bridegroom; "but she is of a higher family than mine, possessing houses, and lands, and property." "Property belongs to God," replied she; and so saying, she retired from the conference. We have since heard that, although the family of the girl is *too respectable* to permit that her betrothed husband should see her face even in her mother's presence, he has put the houses, and lands, and property in the scale, and found her defect too light to be worthy of consideration.

———————

LETTER XVIII.

April, 1843.

MY DEAR FRIEND,

IT is indeed, true, that slavery cannot be presented to the mind but with a revolting aspect; yet I do assure you that slavery in the East is not what you imagine it to be. Here, perhaps, the slave is more in the power of the master than in the West, and there are some monsters, at whose names humanity shudders, who dreadfully abuse the power they legally claim; but, generally speaking, an Eastern slave is exceedingly indulged, and many who have been cruelly torn from their parents at an early age, find and acknowledge fathers and mothers in those to whom they are sold. They are generally extremely well dressed, well fed, and allowed to indulge in a degree of familiarity which would astonish you. If they conduct themselves well, they are frequently married by their masters to persons of respectability, and the ceremony of the marriage of a slave in the high hareems is conducted with extreme magnificence. It is not unusual for a grandee to give away in marriage several female slaves, and sometime concubines ···

the same day, to husbands of his own selection.
In some instances, the slaves are distressed at being
thus disposed of, and would rather remain in their
old home, but generally a marriage of this kind is
a subject for extraordinary rejoicing; and accustomed as the women are to submit to the will of
others in the affair of matrimony, from the highest
to the lowest in the East, the fact of their superiors choosing for them their husbands rather recommends itself to their approval, and excites
their gratitude. On the day of their marriage
they are dressed in the most costly manner;
while in the hareems to which they belong, Cashmere shawls, sometimes cloth of gold, are laid
that they may walk over them. Singing and
dancing women are engaged for the occasion, and
several girls bearing censers, and others sprinkling
perfumes, attend each bride. You have heard and
read of the Arab dancing, which is far from delicate, but the dancing in the Turkish hareems is
not in any respect objectionable. The girls throw
themselves about extravagantly, but frequently
gracefully; and turn heels over head with amusing
dexterity. It is not a pleasing exhibition, but not
a disgusting one.

I cannot admire the singing, the women choose
generally such exceedingly high keys that it resembles screaming rather than singing. I sometimes
think that with the support of a tolerable accom-

paniment the songs might be agreeable, but the instruments of the country are anything but musical, and interfere considerably with the purposes of harmony. The voices of the singers are remarkably fine, and would be perfection under European culture; and the performers are usually enthusiastic in their love for their art, but still more so are their hearers. The vocalists are for the most part respectable.

When the slave of a grandee is given away in marriage, the man chosen as her husband is almost always somewhat of a dependant; and the lady generally treats him as if he were somewhat of a dependant with respect to herself.

I have been exceedingly amused lately, by reading in the " Sketches of Persia," the account which is given by some natives of that country (including persons occupying high offices under government, therefore the noble of the land), of the liberty and power of their women; and I am disposed to think with them, that women, in many respects, have the ascendency among the higher orders throughout the East. We imagine in England that the husband in these regions is really lord and master, and he is in some cases; but you will scarcely believe that the master of a house may be excluded for many days from his own hareem, by his wife's or wives' causing a pair of slippers to be placed outside the door, which si~

nifies that there are visitors within.   It is true that the husband sometimes becomes tired of frequent exclusion, and forbids, as indeed he has a right to do, the constant admission of visitors; but in so doing, he draws down on his head much discomfort.   He has his remedy, certainly; but how sad is the system of divorce!   Who can defend it? Where a wife has become a mother, the husband is seldom willing to divorce her; but where this is not the case, the affair is far too easily managed.

Among the lower orders, some of the husbands are sad tyrants.   The fact is, that the men foolishly marry such little young creatures, they are more like their children than their wives, and their inexperience unjustly provokes their husbands.   While on this subject, it occurs to me to tell you that Deborah has a most refractory grand-daughter, who is certainly the plague of her life.   This child is in the habit of reviling the neighbours' servants; and a few days since she used abusive language to a man who was sitting in his master's doorway.   The doorkeeper was exceedingly provoked, and at once retorted, "When I have a little more money, I will marry you, and punish you every day."   This manner of revenge is something really new to us Europeans.

Last week, a little bride was paraded through the streets in our neighbourhood, whose age could ᵔarcely have exceeded ten years.   Thinking the

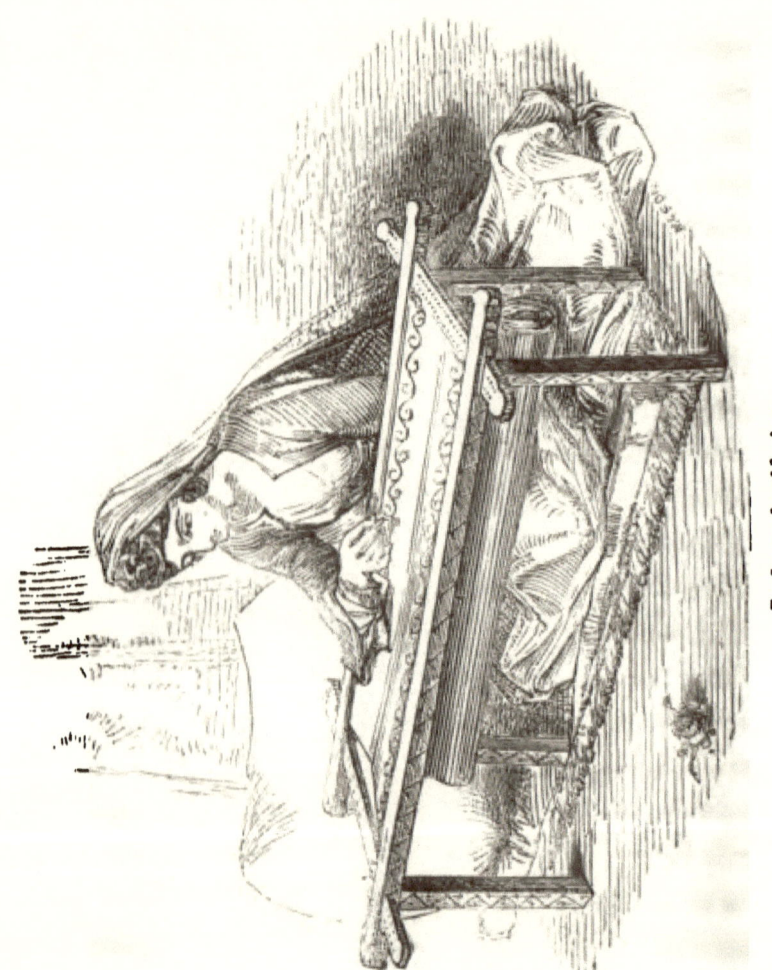

Lady embroidering.

procession, and the whole affair, an exceedingly good joke, she was impatient of control; and instead of walking under the canopy, and submitting to march between two of her female friends, preceded by a woman fanning her, she insisted upon walking backwards before the former, and fanning them herself. This will give you some idea of the mere children who are married here.

The employments of the hareem chiefly consist in embroidery, on an oblong frame, supported by four legs; but they extend to superintending the kitchen, and indeed the female slaves and servants generally; and often ladies of the highest distinction cook those dishes which are particularly preferred. The sherbets are generally made by the ladies; and this is the case in one hareem I visit, where the ladies, in point of rank, are the highest of Eastern *haut ton*. The violet sherbet is prepared by them in the following manner:—The flowers are brought to them on large silver trays, and slaves commence by picking off the outer leaves; the ladies then put the centres of the violets into small mortars, and pound them until they have thoroughly expressed the juice, with which, and fine sugar, they form round cakes of conserve, resembling, when hardened, loaf-sugar dyed green. This produces a bright green sherbet, prettier than the blue or pink, and exceedingly delicate. I do not know of what the blue is composed, but am told that it is a particular preparation of violets; the pink is of roses; the yellow of oranges, apricots, &c.   It would be tedious were I to describe the variety of sherbets; but those I have mentioned will give you an idea of these cooling summer drinks.   About four table-spoonfuls of syrup in three-quarters or a pint of water form a most agreeable beverage.

You will be surprised to hear that the daughter of the Pasha, in whose presence the ladies who attend her never raise their eyes, superintends the washing and polishing of the marble pavements in her palaces.   She stands on such occasions barefooted on a small square carpet; holding in her hand a silver rod: about twenty slaves surround her; ten throw the water, while others follow them wiping the marble, and lastly polishing it with smooth stones.

It is very grievous that the women in general are merely instructed in handiwork.   But I must not speak slightingly of their embroidery; for it is extremely beautiful—as superior as it is unlike to any fancy-work practised in England.   Taste of a very remarkable kind is displayed in its execution; and similar, in many respects, to that exhibited in the most elaborate decorations of Arabian architecture; but its singular beauty is in some measure produced, where colours are employed, by the plan of often taking the colours at random.

Lady w riding.

The embroidery which is done in the hareems is very superior to any other, and frequently interspersed with precious stones, generally diamonds, pearls, emeralds, and rubies. The rich large brocade trowsers often are richly ornamented with jewels, and are stiff with decorations; but the Saltah (a small jacket) for chasteness and elegance is that which I most admire of all the embroidered articles of dress. For winter wear, it is of velvet, or fine cloth, lined with silk. Saltahs of rich silk are worn during the autumn and spring; and, during the summer, dresses of European muslin are almost universally adopted, and are the only kind of apparel suited to the intense heat of an Egyptian summer.

Few of the ladies can read and write even their own language. I know, however, some exceptions. In one family, the daughters have been extremely well instructed by their brother, whose education was completed in Europe. In their library are to be found the works of the first Italian poets and the best literature of Turkey; and these they not only read, but understood.

LETTER XIX.

Cairo, June, 1843.

MY DEAR FRIEND,

THERE has been an alarm of plague in Cairo, and several of the great hareems have been in quarantine. The apprehension has been induced by the fearful murrain which has raged during nine months, as a similar misfortune has proved in former years the forerunner of a severe pestilence.

I mentioned to you some time since that such a calamity was dreaded; and it has in some measure arrived. At El-Mansoorah, the cases of plague have not been few; and while on this subject I must tell you an extraordinary fact, which will show you that it is even possible to extract sweet from one of the bitterest of human draughts. Some Russians have been at El-Mansoorah for the purpose of studying the disease. As a means of discovering whether it be contagious or not, they have employed persons to wear the shirts of the dead, and paid them five piastres a day for so doing. This was a considerable salary, being equal to a shilling per day! Now when the poor of this country consider half a piastre per day a sufficient allowance for each person, and maintain themselves well, in their own opinion, on this trifling sum, you can conceive how charmed they might be with the liberal offers of these Russian gentlemen, were it not for the risk they incurred. Risk, however, they did not imagine. The poor flocked to the physicians from all parts of the town, and *entreated* to be permitted to wear the plague-shirts. One old man urged his request, saying, " I am a poor old man, with a family to maintain; do not refuse me; by your life, let me wear a shirt." The women crowded round the house where their imagined benefactors had taken up their quarters, to bless them for having undertaken to support them, their husbands, and their children: and when the chief of these adventurous gentlemen found the dwelling thus surrounded, he walked forth among them, and, taking off his hat, made a courteous low bow to his dark-eyed visitors; whereupon they made the air resound with the shrill zaghareet, or cries of joy.

Not one of the shirt-wearers died, although the physicians after a short time (during which they awaited the result of their experiment) had recourse to heating the shirts to 60° Réaumur. Still the poor peasants lived, and throve on their good fare; but one of the physicians died. How he

took the disorder is of course a subject for contro-
versy, but that the shirt-wearers escaped, is a great
triumph to the non-contagionists of Cairo; and
from all we can learn, the best informed are of this
party.

In the house of a merchant in Cairo, a slave has
lately died of plague, and, according to custom,
a soldier was placed at the door to enforce strict
quarantine.   The merchant did not relish this
restraint, and desired the comfort of going in and
out at pleasure. Accordingly, he attacked the
cupidity of his temporary gaoler, and coaxingly
addressed him, saying, " Thou knowest, O my
brother, that I am a merchant, and therefore have
much business to transact in the markets, where
my presence is necessary. Let me go, I beseech
thee, and I will hire another to take my place.
Consider my case in thy generosity," he added,
putting into his hand a piece of nine piastres; and
the soldier found his pity so sensibly touched, that
further remonstrance was unnecessary: the merchant passed, and the substitute was accepted—a
new way of keeping quarantine!

Long since I told you that I feared the plague
might induce us, this year, to go to Upper Egypt;
but the accounts have never been such as to show
us the necessity; indeed, on the contrary, though
constantly making the most anxious inquiries, we

did not hear that there had been many cases of plague in the city, until the time of danger had passed.

It is a singular and sad fact, that during our few months' sojourn here this country has been visited by three of its peculiar plagues—murrain, boils and blains (or common pestilence), and locusts. The first has destroyed cattle to an almost incredible amount of value; the second has not been so severe as it usually is; but the locusts are still fearfully eating the fruits of the ground. In the gardens of Ibraheem Pasha and others, the peasants are employed to drive them away by throwing stones, screaming, beating drums, &c.

My assertion with regard to the small daily pay that contents these poor people will show you how much it is in the power of a person of moderate income to dispense comfort to a considerable number of poor grateful fellow-creatures; and could you but see the blind, lame, old people who solicit alms in the streets of Cairo, you would yearn to supply their simple wants.

Those who are above distress are, with the exception of a very small proportion, such as we should number in England among the poor; but, in many respects, they husband their little property in a very strange manner: though they never waste a morsel of food, they are sometimes extravagant with trifles, simply from want of management. A short time since we received from a shop a little parcel about a span long, round which was wound forty-seven feet of string, so that the paper was only here and there visible; and this was not, as you might suppose, on account of the value of its contents, which cost but a few pence.

The climate produces a great degree of lassitude, and the people will often use anything within their reach (if their own property) rather than make the smallest exertion; and yet, as I have remarked to you some time since, no people can work harder or more willingly when called on to do so. I do exceedingly like the Arabs, and quite delight in my rides in remarking the grace and politeness which cast a charm on their manners. It is very interesting to see two peasants meet; there appears so much kindly feeling among them, many good-humoured inquiries ensue, and they part with mutual blessings.

While riding out, a few days since, I was surprised by witnessing the extreme display which is exhibited during the wedding festivities of a mere peasant. When I arrived within a few doors of the house of the bridegroom, I passed under a number of flags of red and green silk, suspended to cords extending across the street; above these were hung seven immense chandeliers, composed of variegated lamps; and awnings of green and white canvas were stretched from roof to roof, and afforded an agreeable shade. Here the bride was paraded, covered with a red Cashmere shawl, numerously attended, and preceded by her fanner, beneath a rose-coloured canopy.

A stranger might imagine that the feast which concludes this display is the result of extreme hospitality, but this is not the case; I was surprised at hearing of the system on which it is conducted. A peasant, for instance, will often buy two sheep, two hundredweight of flour, and butter in proportion; these things forming always the chief articles of a feast prepared for the lower orders in Egypt. He will then add different kinds of fruit according to the season, and abundance of tobacco and coffee; and for the amusement of his visitors, he engages singers, and sometimes dancing-girls. To effect this, he will borrow money, and his next step will be to invite all his relations, and all his friends and acquaintance. These feel obliged to accept the invitation; and no one joins the party without a present in his hand : therefore, at the conclusion of the feast, the bridegroom is often rather a gainer by the festivities than otherwise. In every instance his friends enable him to repay those from whom he has borrowed. Real hospitality has no part in the affair whatever. Ostentation alone. actuates the bridegroom in making his preparations.

On the morning after his marriage he is generally accompanied by his friends into the country, or to a garden, where they feast together, and are usually entertained by dancing and songs. The expense of this *fête champêtre*, in like manner, seldom falls heavily upon the bridegroom.

The Egyptians have an especial passion for gardens and water. Even stagnant water, if sweet, they consider a luxury: running water, however dirty, they hold to be extremely luxurious; and when, during the inundation, the canal of Cairo is full, all the houses on its banks are occupied by persons who sit in their leisure hours smoking by its muddy waters: but the height of their enjoyment consists in sitting by a fountain—this they esteem Paradise.

How much I wish we had the comfort of occasional showers in Egypt: however, one of my boys amuses me often by supplying this desideratum by watering their garden from an upper projecting window; employing for this purpose a large watering-pot with an ample rose, whence many a refreshing shower falls before the lower windows, washing the thick dust from a mulberry-tree, and really giving an agreeable idea of coolness.

This same mulberry-tree was an object of great admiration to a man who described our present house to us before we saw it: he said, after stating the accommodation which the house afforded, " And there is a *tree* in the court!" Having forgotten what sort of tree it was, he blessed the Prophet (as these people do when they want to brush up their memory), and then said, " It is a vine."

This sultry day I can write no more ; and if able to forget the heat, the poor little sparrows would remind me that it is indeed oppressive, for they are flying in and out of our windows with their beaks wide open. They do not seem calculated to bear this intense heat ; and they congregate round their food and water on the terrace, looking so pitiable during a hot wind, that we should like to transport them to England. There, however, I am afraid they would not tenant the houses so fearlessly of harm as they do in Egypt. Here is no wanton cruelty : a great deal of apathy with regard to suffering is apparent in the character of the people ; but I do not think the Arabs, in general, ever inflict an intentional injury.

LETTER XX.

July, 1843.

MY DEAR FRIEND,

SINCE I remarked to you the general cheerfulness which reigns in the hareems I had then seen, I have visited one belonging to a Turkish grandee, which offers a sad exception, and touchingly exhibits a picture of family love and blighted happiness. The old and beloved master of this hareem is under a cloud ; he is suffering the displeasure of the Pasha, and is confined in the state prison. I received a most kind welcome from the ladies of his family. I remarked with regret the depression which weighed down the spirits of all who composed it, and I was shocked to hear from the chief lady that she also was a prisoner, having orders not to quit her house.

She was attired in a kind of morning-dress, of white, embroidered with black ; but wore a splendid kind of crown.* This was composed of diamonds, set in gold, forming flowers, &c.,—the whole being of a convex shape, circular, and about six inches in diameter. It was worn upon the crown

* In Arabic a "Kurs."

of the head, attached to the cap round which the head-kerchief was wound, and had a very rich appearance, the diamonds being so near together, that the interstices only served, like the red gold in which the stones were set, to heighten their brilliancy. At a little distance, the crown seemed like one heap of diamonds.

When this lady referred to her heart's trouble, tears rolled down her cheeks; and I do not think there was one lady or slave present whose eyes were not suffused with tears; one especially interested me, for she was quite unlike any Eastern I have seen, having the complexion and the auburn hair and eyes of the pretty Irish. She manifested by the expression of her countenance more distress than her companions. I imagined she was one of her master's wives; for she was attended by her nurse carrying her child (an exquisite little cherub) and several slaves. She did not, however, sit on the divan by " Hánum," or the chief lady.

The mothers here exceedingly fear the evil or envious eye; and it is quite necessary, when an infant or young child appears, to exclaim, " Máshálláh," and to refrain from remarking its appearance; it is also important to invoke for it the protection and blessing of God; and having done so by repeating the expressive phrases used on such occasions in Eastern countries by Christians as well as Muslims, the parents are happy that their chil-

dren have been introduced to the notice of those
who put their trust in God.

The apartments of this hareem are situated in a
large garden; and the interior decorations are like
those of most Turkish palaces in this country. The
walls are painted in compartments, and adorned
with ill-executed landscapes, representing villas
and pleasure-grounds.

I once told you that in all the hareems I had
seen, the chief lady was the only wife : I can no
longer make such a boast; but look and wonder,
as an Englishwoman, how harmony can exist where
the affection of the husband is shared by —— I do
not like to say how many wives.

Hareem-gardens are never agreeable places of
resort in or near a town; for the walls are so high
that there is no free circulation of air, and the trellises for the support of vines over the walks are
really roofs, necessary certainly at noon-day under
a nearly vertical sun, but excluding the only refreshing morning and evening air.

I was surprised, during my second visit to the
hareem of Habeeb Effendi, to find the ladies (whom
I had not seen for a long time on account of the
late plague) immersed in politics, and painfully
anxious on account of the difference of opinion
which has arisen between the Emperor of Russia
and their cousin the Sultán. They earnestly inquired whether England would espouse the cause

of Turkey, and were in some measure comforted
by a reference to the friendship which England had
so warmly manifested for the young Sultán, and the
active measures which our government had adopted
for the re-establishment of his rule in Syria. I find
the feeling very strong in favour of England in the
hareems; and I conclude that I hear general opinions echoed there.   I judge not only from the remarks I hear, but from the honourable manner in
which I am treated; and the reception, entertainment, and farewell I experience are in every respect highly flattering.

I told you of the great politeness that was shown
me on the occasion of my first visit to the royal
ladies I have just mentioned. On my second visit
to them I was almost perplexed by the honour with
which they distinguished me; for the chief lady
resigned her own place, and seated herself below
me. I was obliged to comply with her desire;
but did so with much reluctance.

I saw nothing that I need describe, in the way
of dress or ornament, on this occasion, excepting
the girdle of the elder daughter. This was a broad
band, of some dull material of a pale grey colour,
embroidered with small white beads, which composed an Arabic sentence, and having a most splendid diamond clasp, in the form of two shells, somewhat wider than the belt.   There was another
visitor present, who by her title and appearance I

saw to be a lady of very high rank; and if the Turks, as some people say, admire fat women, she must be considered a prodigious beauty. I have seldom, if ever, seen a larger person.

One of the most beautiful women I have seen in Egypt is the wife of a celebrated poet. I love to look on a pretty face, and hers is especially sweet. Her manners, too, are charming; her welcome on my introduction was particularly cordial, and her request that I would pay her a long visit was made with evident sincerity of kindness. With the exception of her diamond crown, her dress was simple, and her whole demeanour free from affectation; I should imagine her character is a source of cheerful contentment to her husband and her children. You will forgive my national pride and prejudice when I say she reminded me of an Englishwoman.

The house of this lady's family is of the old Arab description, and is situated on the margin of a lake in the outskirts of the city, surrounded by excellent and very picturesque houses, having, on the ground-floors, courts roofed with trellises, supported by pillars, and other fanciful wood-work, and covered with jasmines and vines. In these the male inhabitants spend their pastime or idle hours, looking on the water. The upper floors are furnished with meshrebeeyehs (the projecting windows I have described to you) overlooking the lake.

From visits I turn to visitors; to tell you that

Egyptian House.

a most unwelcome guest made his appearance yes
terday.   Between the blind and glass of a window
in the room where we usually sit, I discovered a
large snake, more than a yard and a half long.   It
was outside the window; but directly it saw me
through the glass, it raised its head, and protruded
its black forked tongue.   It was of a light brown
colour, and down the centre of its back its scales
were of a bright yellowish hue.   It was in such a
situation that it was scarcely possible to catch it,
and indeed my brother was the only man in the
house who would attempt to do so; for our servants were so overcome by superstitious dread, that
they would not approach the intruder, and one of
the men dared not even look at it : we were therefore unwilling he should touch it, and persuaded
him to send for a snake-charmer.

   There was considerable difficulty in finding, at
such a moment, a man of this profession, although
Cairo abounds with them.   At length a poor old
man arrived, who was nearly blind, and mistook a
towel (which was pressed between the sashes to
prevent the creature entering) for the object of my
dread.   He addressed it with much courtesy, saying " O Blessed !" several times, which expressed
an invitation : to this, however, the snake turned a
deaf ear ; and twining itself dexterously through
the trellis blind, it curled into a window in the
court, and was entirely lost.   We certainly would

rather it had been found, although assured it could only be, from our description, a harmless house-snake.

You have doubtless read many accounts of the feats of Eastern snake-charmers, and wondered at their skill. Very lately, a friend of ours witnessed an instance of the fascination, or rather attraction, possessed by one of these people. He was in the house of an acquaintance when the charmer arrived, who, after a little whistling, and other absurd preliminaries, invoked the snake thus: "I conjure thee, by our Lord Suleymán" (that is, Solomon, the son of David), "who ruled over mankind and the Ján" (or Genii); "if thou be obedient, come to me; and if thou be disobedient, do not hurt me!" After a short pause, a snake descended from a crevice in the wall of the room, and approached the man, who secured it. No other snake appearing, it was decided that the house was cleared, and our friend requested the snake-charmer to accompany him to his own house. He did so, and invoked the snakes in the same words. The invocation was attended by the same result: a snake descended, and in the same manner resigned itself to the serpent-charmer.

With regard to the serpent still in our house, let us say, with the Muslims, we are thankful it is not a scorpion. Their philosophy is a lesson to us.

Several poor neighbours have lately been stung by scorpions: we sent them some carbonate of ammonia to apply to the wounds, and it was the means of producing the happiest results.

Cairo, with its many ruined houses, affords innumerable nests for noxious reptiles; and the progress of its decay has lately been so rapid, that at last a proclamation has been issued by the Pasha for extensive alterations and repairs throughout the city. The houses are to be whitewashed within and without; those who inhabit ruined houses are to repair or sell them; and uninhabited dwellings are to be pulled down for the purpose of forming squares and gardens; meshrebeeyehs are forbidden, and mastabahs are to be removed. Cairo, therefore, will no longer be an Arab city, and will no longer possess those peculiarities which render it so picturesque and attractive. The deep shade in the narrow streets, increased by the projecting windows—the picturesque tradesman, sitting with one friend or more before his shop, enjoying the space afforded by his mastabah—these will be no more; and while I cannot but acknowledge the great necessity for repairing the city, and removing the ruins which threaten the destruction of passengers, I should have liked those features retained which are essentially characteristic—which help, as it were, to group the people, and form such admirable accessories to pictures.

I must add to this letter an account of a shameful and very ridiculous imposition which was practised upon us a fortnight ago. A poor old man who had for some time filled the situation of doorkeeper to our quarter, had long been ill, and had been assisted by several gentlemen in procuring some necessary comforts. One day my brother received a letter from the Sheykh of the quarter, telling him that poor Mohammad the doorkeeper had received mercy at the sixth hour of the preceding night, and expressing a hope that he would give them the price of his shroud. My brother, accordingly, sent one of his servants to the house of Mohammad, where he found his body laid out, a washer of the dead attending, and his wife apparently in great distress on account of her loss. She returned the most grateful acknowledgments for the bounty which was sent to aid in enabling her to bury her poor husband; and after a while the affair passed from our recollection (we never having seen the poor man), or if remembered, it was only to inquire who would supply his place.

The old woman removed to another house a few days after; and a maid-servant of ours, on passing by chance her new dwelling, was surprised to the last degree to see the late doorkeeper sitting within its threshold. "What," exclaimed she, "my uncle Mohammad alive, and well!" "Praise be to God," he answered, "I am well, and have lived on the bounty of your master, the Efendee; but, by your life, my daughter, do not tell him that I am alive." The old man, I should here tell you, is no relation of the maid's; this being one of the usual modes of address among the lower orders. The maid promised his existence should continue a secret; but she found on her return home it was impossible to keep her word, and the quarrel which ensued between her and the servant who conveyed the money for the shroud (both believing their own eyes) was as violent as that between Hároon Er-Rasheed and his wife Zubeydeh, or rather that between their two emissaries, on the subject of Abu-l-Hasan the wag.

LETTER XXI.

September, 1843.

MY DEAR FRIEND,

IN describing to you the honourable reception and elegant entertainment I experienced in the Pasha's hareem, I cannot be too minute.

The chief residence of his ladies is the Kasr ed-Dubárah, a fine house situated on the west of Cairo, on the eastern bank of the Nile, and justly their favourite retreat. After riding through the plantations of Ibraheem Pasha, which almost surround the palace, we arrived at the great gates of the Kasr, through which we entered a long road within the high walls covered with trellis closely interwoven with vines. At the end of this we dismounted, and walked on a beautiful pavement of marble through several paths, until we arrived at the curtain of the hareem. This being raised, we were immediately received by a young wife of Mohammad 'Alee, who addressed my friend Mrs. Sieder in the most affectionate terms, and gave us both a most cordial welcome. In a moment a crowd of ladies assembled round us, vying with each other in paying us polite attention; and

A Turkish Lady in the summer dress of white muslin.

having disrobed me, they followed us (the wife of the viceroy with us leading the way) to the grand saloon.

· This is a very splendid room, paved with marble, as indeed are all the passages, and, I imagine, all the apartments on the ground-floor ; but as several are entirely covered with matting, I cannot assert this to be the case. The pavement in the saloon is simply white marble, the purest and best laid I have seen in the East. The ceiling (which] is divided into four distinct oblong compartments) is painted admirably in stripes of dark and light blue, radiating from gilded centres, from each of which hang splendid chandeliers containing innumerable wax-lights. The corners and cornices are richly decorated. The pavement under the two centre compartments is not matted, but the two ends, to the right and left on entering, are covered with · fine matting, and fitted with crimson divans.

The windows are furnished with white muslin curtains edged with coloured fringe, some pink and some blue. All the looking-glasses (of which there are perhaps six in the saloon) are furnished with festoons and curtains of pink and blue gauze. There is one table with a cover of pink crape embroidered in stripes of gold, and having upon it a large glass case of stuffed birds. On either side of the door are fanciful stands for large square glass lanterns, composed of pillars, round which

are twined artificial flowers. The windows are
European in form, and the hareem blinds are composed of tasteful iron-work; I can scarcely say
filigree, the pattern is too bold. The entire interior decorations are in light and summer taste,
and the saloon charmingly cool.

We crossed to an apartment on the opposite side,
where the same lady placed us on the divan and
seated herself by our side. This room is entirely
covered with matting, and furnished with most
luxurious divans, extending round three sides, not
raised (as is usual) on a frame about a foot or more
in height, but entirely of cotton, forming mat-
tresses two feet in thickness, placed on the ground.
These are covered with very gay chintz, as are
also the cushions which incline against the walls;
and at the right and left upper corners are distinct
square cushions, covered with white muslin embroidered with black braid, and each having back
cushions to correspond. Above all these there is
a row of small cushions, covered with white muslin
and embroidered with black, corresponding in
pattern with the corner seats. The curtains re-
semble those in the saloon.

Here we received coffee, which was handed to
us by the chief lady of the household, the treasurer,
a particularly lady-like person, to whom it was
handed by a lady who bore it on a silver salver,
attended by several others; one carrying the little

coffee-pot in a silver vessel, suspended by chains, and also used as a censer, containing burning charcoal. The whole group was most picturesque, and many of the ladies were fair, young, and beautiful.

The lady of the Páshá then proposed our returning to the saloon, that she might conduct us to the widow of Toosoon Páshá, and to the daughter of Mohammad 'Alee Páshá, who were sitting at the upper corner. I found the former lady seated on a cushion on the ground, next to the right-hand corner, and the daughter of the Viceroy took the seat of honour, which was also a cushion placed on the ground. Numerous ladies and slaves were in attendance; all standing in a line before the edge of the mat.

We were soon joined by another wife of the Páshá, the mother of Mohammad 'Alee Bey (a boy about nine years of age); her designation is "The lady, the mother of Mohammad 'Alee Bey."

It would be a breach of etiquette, and contrary to hareem laws, were I to describe *particularly* the persons of the wives of the Páshá, or any lady after distinguishing her by her name or her situation in a family; but I may in *general* terms express my admiration of the two ladies I have seen, and I think they are the *only* wives of the viceroy. Both are young—the one is a dignified

and handsome person, and the other especially
gentle and very lovely.

Soon after noon, dinner was announced; and the
widow of Toosoon Páshá led the way to a room
adjoining the saloon, where a most elegant dinner
was arranged, on a very large round silver tray,
placed on a stool, and surrounded by cushions.
The passages we passed were occupied by innumerable black female slaves, and some eunuchs,
dressed in all the variety of gay Eastern costume,
and forming a curious contrast and a most picturesque back-ground to the ladies and white slaves
who surrounded and accompanied us. On either
side of the door several ladies, each with an embroidered napkin hung on her right arm, held
silver ewers and basins that we might wash our
hands before advancing to the table.

No one was admitted to the table but the widow
of Toosoon Páshá, the daughter of Mohammad
'Alee Páshá, the mother of Mohammad 'Alee
Bey, with ourselves, and a lady of great importance
in the East, the foster-mother of 'Abbás Páshá.*
The place of the younger wife was vacant.

The tray was covered with small silver dishes
filled with various creams, jellies, &c., and most
tastefully garnished with exquisite flowers. In the
centre was a fore-quarter of lamb, on piláv. I

---

* 'Abbás Páshá is the reputed successor to the Páshálik.

was truly glad, on this occasion especially, that my home-habits had been Eastern; had the case been otherwise, a joint of meat to be eaten without knife or fork would have been a formidable object; for, under any circumstances, I should not have anticipated that the widow of Toosoon Páshá, who is also the mother of Abbás Páshá, and who, being the eldest, was the most honoured at table, would have distinguished me as she did, by passing to me, with her own fingers, almost every morsel that I ate during dinner. The mother of Moham-mad 'Alee Bey in the same manner distinguished Mrs. Sieder.

The lamb was succeeded by stew; the stew by vegetables; the vegetables by savoury cream, &c., composing an innumerable variety; and each was removed, and its place filled, when perhaps only tasted. Sweet dishes, most delicately pre-pared, succeeded these in rapid succession; and, with one exception, all were in silver dishes. Ladies attended close to our divan with fly-whisks; behind them about thirty formed a semicircle of gaily-dressed, and, in many cases, beautiful women and girls; and those near the door held large silver trays, on which the black slaves who stood without placed the dishes, that the table might be constantly replenished.

Black female slaves in the houses of the great are not permitted to enter an apartment where are

visitors; but black eunuchs, when favourites with
their masters, are constantly to be found in the
very centre of a high hareem.

In presenting the morsels to me, the widow of
Toosoon Páshá constantly said, "In the name of
God;" and these words are always said by the
Muslims before eating or drinking. "Praise be
to God" is the grace after either.

There is one particularly agreeable custom observed after dinner in the East; each person is
at liberty to leave the table when satisfied. To a
European it is really a relief to do so, the dishes
are so numerous, varied, and rich.

There is much grace in the manners of the ladies
of the East even in the most trifling actions: it
was pretty to observe the elegance with which the
silver ewers and basins were held for us when we
left the tray. We were succeeded at the table by
the highest ladies of the household; and I imagine
others, according to their rank, dined after these,
until all had taken their meal.

We returned to the saloon, where we were met
by the younger wife of the Páshá, who had been
prevented joining us at table by indisposition. She
gave me a most kind general invitation to the
Kasr ed-Dubárah, and a particular one to a festival
which is to take place on the occasion of a grand
marriage some time before I quit this country.
The fantasia, she assured me, is to be the most

splendid that can be prepared or arranged; and I shall soon be permitted to tell you the name of the bride. This she told me; but I must not mention it until the day is fixed for the marriage. It is an Egyptian state-secret!

There are many extremely beautiful women in the hareem of the Páshá, and many handsome young girls; some not more than ten years of age. The Turkish ladies, and the Circassians, and Georgians, are generally extremely fair; and I must particularly mention one who was remarkably beautiful, and more splendidly dressed than any of her companions. She did not enter the saloon until we heard dinner announced; and her appearance was something very attractive. Her yelek and shintiyan (or long vest and trousers) were of rich plum-coloured silk, and the quiet colour of her dress exhibited with brilliant effect a profusion of costly diamond ornaments. Her head-dress was tastefully arranged, and the richer sprays of diamonds were lavishly interspersed in a dark crape headkerchief.

I cannot take a better opportunity of describing the Eastern dress, as worn by the Turkish ladies, than while the hareem of the Páshá is fresh in my recollection. The tarboosh (or red cap) is trimmed with a very large and full tassel of dark blue silk, which is separated and spread over the crown, and those ladies who wear rich ornaments almost always display their most costly jewels on the back of the

head, either in the form of a kurs, which I have
described to you, or a spray, very much resembling
in form a *fleur de lis*, but broader and shorter ; this
is placed at the division of the tassel, which latter is
often so broad when spread, as to extend an inch
beyond the head on either side in a front view.
The headkerchief is wound round the head, partly
over the forehead, and the fringed ends are arranged
on one side ; the front hair is cut short, and combed
towards the eyebrows, and this is extremely un-
becoming, disfiguring even a beautiful face, excepting in cases where the hair curls naturally, and
parts on the forehead.   The long hair is disposed
in numerous small plaits, and looped up on either
side over the headkerchief.   In many cases, the
hair of the younger ladies, and white slaves, is dis-
hevelled, and hanging loosely on the shoulders ;
but this I have only observed in the Turkish
hareems : many in the Kasr ed-Dubárah wear their
long hair flowing on their shoulders, and, in
some instances, their attractions are considerably
heightened by this simplicity ; but no *coiffure*,
however studied, or simple, is so pretty as that
worn by the Arab ladies, whose long hair hanging
down the back is arranged in many small plaits
often lengthened by silk braid, and generally adorned
with hundreds of small gold ornaments, resembling
oval spangles, which harmonize better with the
Eastern costume than any other fashion.

To return to the Turkish ladies: they wear the yelek considerably longer than their height; the back part resting on the ground, and forming a graceful train; and in walking over a mat or carpet, they hold the skirts in front over the arm. The shirt is of silk gauze, fine muslin, or a very beautiful thin crape, with glossy stripes, which is made of raw silk in the hareems, and is cream colour: the sleeves of this are not confined at the wrist. The shintiyán are extremely full, and generally of a different material from the yelek: the former being of rich brocade, large patterned muslin, or chintz, or sometimes of plain satin, or gros de Naples. The yelek, on the contrary, is made of a material with a delicate pattern, generally a small stripe, whether of satin, Indian silk, or muslin.

Those ladies who are not perfectly idle, and who have not slaves as train-bearers, tuck their skirts through their girdles; and thus, I think, the dress is very gracefully worn. Ladies of distinction always wear Cashmere shawls round the waist, generally red; and those in Kasr ed-Dubárah had a narrow edge of gold, with gold cords and tassels at the corners. There, the nurz were different from any I had before seen; being of embroidered cloth, of various colours; and the daughter of the Páshá, and others, had their long sleeves buttoned at the wrist. The sleeves are always so made that they can be buttoned if their length prove inconvenient; but as the great ladies of the land do not occupy themselves in any way, but spend their time on their divans, they can scarcely find these hanging draperies incommodious.

This description of dress leads me back to the lady whose appearance so especially attracted my admiration. After I requested that my riding-dress might be brought, I observed several ladies crossing the saloon, among whom she walked, bearing it towards me, and looking like a queen in person and in dress. She dressed me with much grace, and then with her companions stepped back into the doorway to receive and give the parting salutation. One circumstance I have omitted, namely, the crimson embroidered curtains, which hang before all the doorways in the palace; for the doors stand open, a closed door being never permitted in the hareems. Much taste is displayed in the embroidery of these curtains; indeed, the perfection of taste is to be found in the decorations of the Kasr ed-Dubárah.

The Door-curtains.

Letter XXII.

December, 1843,

My dear Friend,

I cannot better give you an idea of the order and discipline observed in the hareems of the great and wealthy than by comparing each to a petty state, with its rulers and its officers. The person occupying the place of highest rank, next to the master, is the chief lady, who is often called, properly or improperly, Hánum, or, correctly, Khánum. This title, which literally signifies 'My Lord,' (for Turkish ladies, whom we in England generally look upon as persons treated with little respect, are honoured with male titles) by right belongs first only to those ladies of the Sultán whom we call sultanas; that is, to any of the near female relations of the sovereign, and to any of his ladies who has borne a prince or princess; secondly, to the wives of the grand vezeer; but it is sometimes given by courtesy to the wives of grandees in general, and sometimes to ladies of inferior grades. The male title Efendim (literally 'My Master') is also given to the same ladies.

The chief lady of the hareem is the mother of

the master; or, if his mother be not living, his sister, or sisters, take precedence; and next to them ranks his favourite wife. The question of priority among the wives of one man is more easily arranged than you, with European notions respecting the rights of women, could imagine possible. It is generally settled thus: the first wife, if she become a mother, retains her rank above any wife subsequently taken; but if not, she yields to another more fortunate, and consequently, more beloved and honoured. The other wives take their stations according to the preference of their husbands.

Each wife, among the higher classes, has her separate apartments, and distinct attendants; for *even Eastern* wives might manifest jealousy under circumstances of constant intercourse with each other. In the cases of the great, it is not unusual for each wife to occupy a separate mansion; but whether in one large house, or several smaller ones, the hareem of the grandee occupies the whole, or nearly the whole, of the abode, which is generally enclosed by garden walls as lofty as the houses in the immediate neighbourhood. Without the aid of scaling ladders, or the more effectual mean of admission —intrigue, the hareem of the Turkish grandee is well secured from illicit visitors. At the outer door is stationed a bowáb, or door-keeper, and the second is guarded by eunuchs. Beyond the second is suspended the hareem curtain which I have be-

fore described; and in the first of the inner apartments are the black female slaves who undertake
the menial offices of the hareem. After passing
the outer apartments white slaves are found carrying silver sprinkling bottles of scented water,
small silver censers suspended by chains, coffee,
pipes, sherbet, and sweetmeats; each set of coffee-
cups or sherbet-cups being placed on a small tray,

Coffee Service.

and often concealed beneath a round splendidly
embroidered cover, bordered with deep and heavy
gold fringe. Among the white slaves may be observed several who are considered superior to their
companions, walking about as though superintending their arrangements; and among the former,
especially, I have found the most lovely girls in
the hareems, many of them fully justifying my pre-

conceived ideas of the celebrated Georgian and Circassian women. Excepting in two cases, cheerfulness has appeared to me to reign among these fair prisoners; entirely excluded as they are from intercourse with any persons of the other sex, except their master and his very near relations. If any other man attempted to pass beyond the first entrance, his temerity would in all probability be punished with death the moment his purpose should be discovered.

The houses of the grandees, separate from their hareems, are generally accessible; and the liberty of ingress is sometimes not a little abused. Last month Mohammad 'Alee was residing in his palace at Shubra, and two Europeans resorted thither for the purpose of seeing the gardens. They wore the Frank dress, with the exception of their having adopted the tarboosh, a shawl round the waist, and red shoes. After perambulating the gardens, they entered the palace, and meeting with no opposition, they examined one apartment after another, and at length entered the bedroom of the Páshá, where sat his highness, nearly undressed! Although taken by surprise, his Turkish coolness did not forsake him : calling for his dragoman, he said, " Enquire of those gentlemen where they bought their tarbooshes." The Europeans replied, " They were purchased in Constantinople;" " and *there*," rejoined the Páshá, " I suppose they learned their

manners. Tell them so." Judging from this retort
that their presence was not agreeable, the Franks
saluted the viceroy, and withdrew.

This reminds me of another late occurrence, in
which, however, was exhibited only a want of
knowledge of Turkish etiquette; no absence of
gentlemanly mind. An European gentleman who
lately visited Egypt was introduced, among others
in this city, to a grandee, and was accompanied to
his residence by a friend of my brother, and Mons.
L——, both of whom, during many years, have
resided in this country, and visited in the best
Eastern society. After they had partaken of the
usual refreshment of pipes and coffee, sherbet was
brought, and handed first to the stranger. He
looked at it for a moment, and then at the gaily
embroidered napkin hung over the arm of the slave
who presented it; and following the impulse given,
I conclude by his preconceptions of Eastern habits
of cleanliness, dipped his fingers in the sweet beverage, and wiped them on the napkin. Mons.
L——, with the perfect delicacy which characterises French politeness, followed his example,
dipped his fingers in the sherbet, and wiped them
on the napkin. I wonder whether their host understood his motive for such strange doings. My
brother's friend sat at a little distance from his companions, and confessed that he drank his sherbet.

To return to the organization of the great ha-

reems: the Hánum generally has four principal
attendants, two of whom are elderly, and act simply
as companions: the third is the treasurer, and the
fourth, the sub-treasurer. The next in rank are
those who hand pipes and coffee, sherbet and sweetmeats; and each of these has her own set of sub-
ordinates. Lastly rank the cooks and house-slaves,
who are mostly negresses. The hareem is a little
world of women, in which many have passed their
infancy and their childhood; the scene of their
joys and sorrows, their pleasures and their cares;
beyond which, they have no idea of a wider theatre
of action; and from which they anticipate no
change but to the hareem of their husbands.

The ideas entertained by many in Europe of the
immorality of the hareem are, I believe, erroneous.
True it is, that the chief ladies have much power
which they might abuse; but the slaves of these
ladies are subject to the strictest surveillance; and
the discipline which is exercised over the younger
women in the Eastern hareem can only be compared to that which is established in the convent.
A deviation from the strictest rules of modesty is
followed by severe punishment, and often by the
death of the delinquent. The very framework of
Eastern society is so opposed to the opinions of
Europeans, that I will venture to prophecy it must
be the work of several generations to root up prejudice before the mind of the Eastern can be pre-

pared for the reception of our ideas of civilization.
That Christianity is the only medium through
which happiness may be attained by any people is
most certain; therefore as the Easterns are very
far from being Christians, except in the mere
dogmas of their faith (inasmuch as they acknowledge the Messiah, though denying his divine nature, and his atonement for sin), so they are very
far from being really happy.

The prejudice existing among the Turkish
women against the pure doctrines of Christianity
is evident from occasional, or rather, I should say,
from frequent remarks made in my presence, and
to my friends.   One lady, who gave me a general
and warm invitation to her hareem, and treated me
really affectionately, so far betrayed her opinions,
that she exclaimed to me, and to my friend, " What
a pity that you are Christians!"   Alas! such
feelings are too general for our minds to be blinded
to the fact of their existence ; and so long as martyrdom awaits the convert to our blessed faith,
little or no progress will be made by those benevo-
lent men, whose devotion of happiness and of life
to our Saviour's cause will secure for them the
favour of their God, however unsatisfactory may
be the results of their labours.

Of those female slaves who, after the age of
childhood, have been brought from countries where
they have enjoyed almost unbounded liberty, few,

perhaps, become reconciled to confinement within the narrow and limited precincts of the hareem. Some, by their personal charms rendered favourites of the master, doubtless delight in the luxurious prison. Others, who have, in addition to his favour and affection, a stronger tie to their foreign home—that of their having borne him a child, would receive their emancipation, if accompanied by a dismissal and a marriage to some other person, with earnest prayers for the retraction of the intended boon. Brought up, in general, with Muslim feelings, they become the most affectionate of mothers. Their maternal tenderness is often most especially manifested by their dread of the evil eye; a superstition which obliges me, in my intercourse with Muslim mothers, to observe the utmost caution in making any remarks upon children.

In one instance, I was unfortunate, in one respect, in a remark of this kind; but fortunate in another respect, inasmuch as one of my own children was the subject. I occasioned much distress to an Arab lady who was passing the day with me (when, in the course of conversation, the effects of climate on the constitution of the young were discussed) by observing that my eldest boy had not suffered as the rest of our party had done from the heat; adding thankfully, that I considered him strong. In an instant she vociferated, " Bless the

Prophet! bless the Prophet!" and repeated this for some time, while she coloured deeply, and exhibited the most extraordinary agitation. I confess I was at first confounded; for although I perceived that in her enthusiasm she feared that I had endangered my dear boy's welfare by expressing my opinion of his health, and that she earnestly desired I should avert any calamity by doing as she directed at the moment, I was not at all disposed to *bless the Prophet;* but I endeavoured to quiet her apprehensions by repeating in Eastern phraseology " Praise be to God for the health of my family," and " If it please God may it continue." Finding me calmly and gravely endeavouring to convince her that the English do not fear expressing their satisfaction in the welfare of those they love, she became more tranquil, but I do not think she felt reassured. By saying " O God, bless our Lord Mohammad !" the effect of the evil eye is believed to be prevented; and it is not a little singular, that my friend feared the effect of my own admiring eye, upon my own child.

It is very difficult for a stranger, like myself, to avoid making mistakes in various other ways. For example, I heard footsteps on the stairs leading to our terrace a few days since, and beckoned a maid, who was passing, that she might inquire for me who was gone up stairs, when, to my astonishment, she ran from me immediately; and though I called

her by name, and induced her to look round, she
saw me again beckoning with my hand, and continued her flight. Annoyed at what appeared to
be perverseness, I clapped my hands, and she at
once returned. " Why did you run away when I
beckoned you ?" said I.   " Because," replied she,
" you made a signal to me to go away." That is,
I turned towards her the back of my hand. Had
I reversed the position, or beckoned with the palm
downwards, she would have understood that I
wanted her; as it was, she supposed that she was
to run away as fast as possible.

I do not remember that I mentioned to you the
uncouth dresses that are worn here at this season
of the year by the ladies of the higher classes.
When I pay an unexpected visit to such persons, I
generally find most of them in quilted jackets of a
description as little becoming as can be imagined,
or enveloped in any warm covering that they have
at hand. Their rooms are warmed by means of
the brazier, which produces a close and suffocating
smell, such as I cannot easily endure ; and, indeed,
I seldom feel much occasion for a fire. The weather is now really delightful; but it has not been
so uniformly since the commencement of winter.
As in the cases of most travellers, our residence
here has been marked by peculiarities. The extraordinary inundation of last year, and the heavy
rain of this, are events which have had no pre-

cedents on record during the lives of the present
generation. After wishing for occasional showers
during eight months in vain, not a drop of rain
falling, we had on the thirtieth of October a tremendous storm of rain, attended with thunder and
lightning, and one almost continuous peal of thunder lasted two hours, rattling and rolling in a most
awful manner, while the rain fell in torrents; but
on the first of last month, the rain was still more
copious: it poured through the roofs and ceilings;
and we and our servants during the storm were
seeking dry corners in which to deposit cushions,
mattrasses, and other furniture; and were running
hither and thither to remove them as the water
gained upon us. Our house is extremely well-
built for Cairo, and yet, in the upper rooms,
pretty smart showers fell through the ceilings for
some time after the storm abated, and only one
room in the house escaped the general flooding.
Our poor neighbours suffered severely, and fearful
has been the illness which has ensued; indeed, the
inhabitants are still feeling lamentably the effects
of that tremendous storm. Many houses have
fallen in consequence of it; and others have been
greatly injured. The roofs, in many instances, are
seldom plastered with anything better than mud,
but simply composed of planks and strong beams,
on which coarse matting is laid; and often over
all only rubbish is strewed to preserve the matting

from being blown away: therefore the showers which penetrate these roofs sometimes become showers of mud, to the destruction of furniture. Rain, however, seldom falls in this part excepting in the cooler season, when a few showers occur, and those are generally light.

LETTER XXIII.

January, 1844.

My dear Friend,

I was presented yesterday to Nezleh Hánum, by my friend Mrs. Sieder. My reception was remarkably flattering, and perhaps unusually so, because it took place in her bed-room. I was not aware that she was suffering from severe indisposition when I called at the Kasr ed-Dubárah, and would not have intruded when I was informed that this was the case; but when she heard that I had arrived, she expressed her desire to see me as soon as her two physicians, then in attendance, should have quitted her chamber. Her highness is the eldest daughter of the Páshá, and therefore holds the highest rank among the ladies of Egypt. I have before said that she is the widow of the Deftardár Mohammád Bey.

While we were sitting in one of the rooms opening into the saloon, the curtain before our door was suddenly closed; for the physicians were passing. In a few minutes the curtain was withdrawn, and I was conducted to the presence of her highness. She was supported by pillows, and evidently

suffering much from cough, and oppression of the
chest.   She received me with much affability, and
at once requested me to sit by her side on a raised
divan, which I imagine is her bed.   Low divans
surrounded the room, and the pavement was covered
with a Turkey carpet.   It had in no respect the
character of a bed-room, but rather that of a luxu-
riously furnished Turkish winter sitting-room.   It
opens into a noble saloon, over that which I formerly described to you.   I found the youngest son
of the Páshá, Mohammad 'Alee Bey, sitting on a
cushion at the feet of his sister, Nezleh Hánum,
and finding me to be unacquainted with Turkish,
he politely conversed with me in French.   He is
nine years of age, and in a few months will be
considered beyond the hareem age.   His mother,
and other ladies, sat on my left hand.   Thus I saw,
on the one hand, a lady about fifty years of age—
the daughter of the Páshá, and on the other, a very
lovely young woman, step-mother to her highness,
the wife of her father, and the mother of her little
brother.

Her highness, in features, and especially in her
eyes, bears a strong resemblance to her father,
having a countenance full of intelligence, and
capable of the most varied expression ; generally
quick and searching in glance ; but often beaming
upon me with the sweetest smile imaginable.   She
directed one of the Páshá's favourites, the mother

of two of his children, to wait upon me.* This
lady received the coffee from another at the entrance
of the chamber, and handed it to me in an exquisite
gold zarf, richly set with rows of large and small
diamonds, arranged spirally, and ornamented between the rows with most delicate enamel. Yesterday was the fourth day of the Great 'Eed, or
Great Beirám (the latter of the two principal
annual festivals of the Muslims), and a day appropriated to visits of ceremony to her highness by
those ladies who have access to her; the three preceding days having been spent by them in visiting
the tombs of relations and friends. While I was
sitting with her, many ladies came in to pay their
respects to her; but in consequence of her illness,
they were simply dressed, with the exception of
one lady, who was most splendidly attired. She
had on the back of her head a profusion of diamonds, and wore a long orange-coloured Cashmere
jubbeh, richly embroidered, and forming, as she
walked, a glittering train of gold. She only
kissed the border of her highness's robe, and left
the room without speaking; none of her visitors
did more than kiss her hand; nor did any one of
them speak a single word; neither did Nezleh
Hánum take any notice of their salutation, otherwise than by allowing them to take her hand.

---

* She has lost both her children.

This etiquette, I am informed, is not only observed during her illness, but at all times. The visitors never raised their eyes; and here I felt peculiarly the advantage of being an Englishwoman, for she kept up with me a lively conversation, and really treated me as an equal. With true Eastern politeness, her highness assured me that our presence made her feel really well; and begged I would consider her house my own; using every persuasion to induce us to prolong our visit. Sherbet was handed to us in deep purple cups, exceedingly elegant, and containing a very delicious beverage. I need only say of the sherbet and coffee covers, and the napkins, that they were as splendid as the most exquisite embroidery could render them; but I must notice her highness's pipes. The mouthpieces were most tastefully adorned with brilliants, set in rich patterns, and the silk covering of each was elaborately decorated with embroidery. She smoked incessantly; but was the only lady in the room who did so. By the way, I have become quite reconciled to sitting among those who smoke, for the scent of the tobacco used by the ladies here is extremely mild, and quite unlike what offends my sex so much in England.

Nezleh Hánum requested me three times to remain when I proposed leaving her, and when at length I urged that I must depart, as it was near sunset, she bade me farewell in the most flattering terms she could employ. On quitting her chamber, I found the lady next in rank to her who handed me the coffee and sherbet, waiting with another cup of sherbet for me to take *en passant*. I mention this because it is always intended as a distinguishing mark of honour. Several ladies accompanied us to the door, and the treasurer followed me with the present of an embroidered handkerchief from her highness.

. Do not think me egotistical, because I describe thus minutely my reception : I consider it important in a description of manners, especially as the receiving and paying visits is the every-day business of an Eastern lady ; and by thus entering into detail, I hope to give an idea of the extreme politeness which characterises those with whom I am acquainted. I may also add, that I think it due to the hareem of the Páshá, and others of distinction, to show the respect they manifest towards the English. Were I a person of rank, there would be nothing remarkable in the honourable attentions I receive ; but as a private lady, I confess they are exceedingly beyond my anticipations. On quitting the Kasr, my attention was attracted by one of the most perfect visions of loveliness I have had the gratification of seeing, in the person of a white slave-girl about seventeen years of age. She stood leaning her head against the doorway, while the line of beauty was described to perfection in the

grace of her attitude : her complexion was delicately fair ; and her hair and eyes were neither of
them dark, but of that gentle shade of brown
which harmonises so charmingly with a fair complexion. I cannot minutely describe her features ;
for there is a perfection of beauty which defies
description, and such was her's. There was an
expression of melancholy on her sweet countenance,
and something so impressive in her appearance,
that those who have seen her once cannot forget
her.

I fear that I shall not soon receive my summons
to the wedding in the Páshá's hareem. There
seems to be some cause for delay which I do not
know ; and it is a subject respecting which I cannot, consistently with politeness, ask any questions
of those who are able to give me the desired
information ; but a cousin of the Sultán told me, a
few days ago, with the utmost gravity, in allusion
to this affair, that there remained *one point* unset-
tled, namely, *the choice of a bridegroom!* Everything else was arranged. Among the great, in
this part of the world, the wishes of a daughter
who is to be given away in marriage seem to be
very seldom considered. She is nourished and
brought up in the expectation of a day when she
will be delivered over by her parents to the protection of a husband, a stranger to her both in
person and in mind. You may well wonder that

A Marriage.

such conduct can be tolerated in any land; and may sigh for those helpless women who are disposed of in this manner; but the reform of such a practice, under present circumstances, is impossible; for I am perfectly confirmed in my opinion that the women themselves would shrink with horror at the proposal to make an intended husband personally acquainted with his wife before the marriage.

Marriages among the middle classes in this city are often conducted with much display of a most singular kind. A bridal procession which passed a few days ago through the principal streets in our neighbourhood, was headed by a fool, or buffoon, who, mounted on a horse, and attired in the most grotesque manner, with a high pointed cap, and a long false beard, performed a variety of ridiculous antics. Two men upon camels, each beating a pair of kettle-drums, of enormous but unequal dimensions, attached to the saddles, immediately followed the fool. Then came a man bearing a cresset, formed of a long pole, having at the top several receptacles for flaming wood, which were covered with embroidered handkerchiefs. This cresset, the proper use of which is to serve as a light at night, was thus used merely for display. Next came a man on tall stilts, and two swordsmen gaily attired in cloth of gold, brandishing drawn swords, and occasionally engaging in a mock fight. The swordsmen were succeeded by

Men with Cressets.

two dancing men, and these by vocal and instru-
mental musicians, singing and playing with the
utmost vigour. Then followed five boys, each
about five or six years of age, attired in female
apparel of the richest description, heavy with gold,
and decorated with a profusion of women's ornaments composed of gold and costly jewels, which
dazzled the sight. These boys were being paraded
previously to circumcision; and each of them

partly covered his face with a folded embroidered handkerchief, to guard against the evil eye. They were followed by four women, whose office had been to summon the female friends to the wedding. Each of these, who, like all who followed them, were on foot, had a rich piece of cloth of gold thrown over her left shoulder, with the edges attached together on her right side. The pieces of cloth were presents which they had received. About thirty young girls, all veiled and handsomely dressed, and then about the same number of married ladies (the latter of whom, enveloped in their black silk habarahs, looked, to the eye of a European, as if they were attired rather for a funeral rather than for a wedding) followed next; and then came the bride. She was entirely covered by a rich Cashmere shawl, as usual; but upon that part of it which covered her head-dress and bridal crown were attached such splendid jewelled ornaments as are seldom seen except in the hareems of grandees. Attended by two female relations, one on each side of her, followed by others, and preceded by a woman, who walked backwards, constantly fanning her (notwithstanding the coldness of the weather) with a large fan of black ostrich-feathers, she walked under a canopy of yellow gauze, supported by four poles, at the upper ends of which were attached embroidered handkerchiefs. Behind this walked a band of musicians. The whole was like one of those scenes described in the Thousand and One. Nights; so gay, so brilliant, and so strikingly Eastern. The procession advanced almost as slowly as a tortoise.

While on the subject of processions and marriage, I may mention a late ridiculous occurrence, arising out of a matrimonial case. Four lawyers of our neighbourhood were last week condemned to hard labour, and paraded through the streets on asses, with their faces towards the tails, for illegal conduct in a suit respecting a refractory wife. In illustration of their offence, I may remind you of a case, which I heard referred for judgment to our neighbour Deborah; that of a young man who agreed to take as his bride a girl reported to have but one eye, because she was a person of property. He did take her, and expended an extravagant sum upon the wedding festivities; but the affair did not end as he expected. He found his wife to be about thirteen years of age, a little delicate child; but possessing some spirit; for she positively and obstinately refused to acknowledge him as her husband. Having been legally married, he could only divorce her, or cause her to be registered as refractory; and he adopted the latter course; in consequence of which he is not obliged to support the girl, her family doing so until she shall resign herself to him. Cases of this kind are of frequent occurrence, and though it often happens that a woman twenty years of age submits without a murmur to be married to a man of threescore, a girl who has not long passed the commencement of her 'teens' very seldom will accept a husband whose chin shows him to be a man.

LETTER XXIV.

February, 1844.

MY DEAR FRIEND,

MY brother's account of the hareem, and all that he has written respecting the manners and customs of the women of this country, I have found to be not only minutely accurate, but of the utmost value to me in preparing me for the life which I am now leading. His information, however, on these subjects, being derived only from other men, is, of course, imperfect; and he has anxiously desired that I should supply its deficiencies, both by my own personal observation, and by learning as much as possible of the state and morals of the women, and of the manner in which they are treated, from their own mouths.

When my experience with respect to the hareem was much shorter as to time, and more limited as to its objects, than it has now been, I was unwilling to express to you an opinion with which I was forcibly impressed within a few months after my arrival in this country; that a very large proportion of the men, and not a few of the women, are frequently, and almost habitually, guilty of the most abominable acts of cruelty and oppression. Though I have seen much that is amiable in the persons with whom I am acquainted here, the opinion above expressed has been so frequently and strongly confirmed that I cannot withstand the conviction of its being correct.

The wives and female slaves, in the houses of the higher orders, are generally, if I may judge from what I have seen and heard, treated by the husband and master with much kindness; and the condition of the slaves seems to be, in one respect, preferable to that of the wives; as the latter are often in constant fear of being divorced; while the sale of a slave who has been long in a family, unless on account of pecuniary distress, is reckoned highly disreputable; and if she have borne a child to her master, and he acknowledge it to be his own, to sell her is illegal. But among the middle and lower classes, both wives and female slaves are often treated with the utmost brutality: the former are often cruelly beaten; and the latter, not unfrequently, beaten to death!

A neighbour of ours, a few weeks ago, flogged his wife in a most barbarous manner, and turned her out of doors, because his supper was not ready precisely at the time appointed. Two days after, however, he brought her back. The same man, not long since, beat a female slave so severely, that she lingered in great pain for about a week, and then died. This man is a Copt, by profession a Christian! Another man beat one of his female slaves until she threw herself from a window, and thus killed herself on the spot. This man also is of the same profession! Much are they mistaken who say, " What need is there of missionaries here to instruct the Copts, who are a Christian people?" One who knows them well assures me that their moral state is far worse than that of the Muslims ; that in the *conduct* of the latter there is much more Christianity than is exhibited in that of the former. But the remarks which I am making apply to both the Muslims and the nominal Christians, but to these are more extensively applicable. How sad that the duty of regarding truth should oblige me to make such a distinction! - The English Institution in this city, the chief object of which is to introduce among the Copts that sound knowledge which is the first requisite to improve their religious and moral condition, I look upon as one of the most useful of all the establishments of the Missionary Society. The accounts of it which have appeared in the publications of that Society have scarcely shown its full importance ; for this cannot be duly appreciated by any one who does not know by experience the state of the people whom it is designed to benefit, and the admirable judgment and indefatigable and self-denying zeal with which its objects are pursued.

Connected with this Institution is a chapel, sufficiently large and very commodious and comfortable, where I am thankful to have opportunities to join in the service of our Church, and to hear many an excellent sermon. But I must return from this digression, to resume the subject which occasioned it.

Seldom do many days elapse without our hearing the most piteous screams from women and children suffering under the whip or stick; and much trouble do we experience in our endeavours to stop the barbarities practised in our immediate neighbourhood. The answer usually returned to our messages of reproach on these occasions are of the most civil kind, assuring us, with many salutations, that, *for our sakes*, the offender shall be forgiven. I believe that the cruelty which now seems so common may, in some degree, be attributed to the oppression which its exercisers themselves suffer; for every one who has studied the human mind will agree with me, that, with few exceptions, the oppressed become the hardest of oppressors.

The women generally seem full of kind and tender feeling, although (as I have remarked) there are not a few instances of the reverse, and lately we have been distressed by the conduct of two women, our near neighbours. The one, old Deborah, whom I mentioned to you in a former letter, has so cruelly beaten a little girl who lives with her, on three or four occasions, that we have taken the poor child into our house each time until she has, by her own choice, returned, when her cruel mistress, who is said to be her grandmother, has promised us not to repeat her violence.

The other was a more distressing case. A woman residing in a house adjoining our own had lost seven piastres, and discovering that a little grandson had stolen them, she sent for a man, by profession a *beater*, to chastise him. One of my boys heard this; and finding that by mounting a little ladder he could reach a window commanding the court of this woman's house, he did so, and immediately called to tell me that the report was a true one; that the man had arrived, and was tying the arms and legs of the poor child; but that his grandmother was standing by him. That being the case, I assured my boy that her only object could be to frighten the child by confining his limbs, and that I felt certain she could not suffer him to be hurt. I formed this opinion from my love for the grandmothers of England, whose children's children are the crown and glory of their age. Alas! for my mistake in supposing this Arab possessed the feelings of woman's nature! I hardly left the foot of the ladder, when I was recalled by the screams of my own dear child, who was crying and scolding in an agony of distress; for the man in the court below was beating the limbs,

the back, the chest of the poor little boy, as in
writhing and rolling on the ground each part fell
under the dreadful blows of a ponderous stick,
while between each infliction the old woman cried
"again!" This brutality could not be suffered,
and my brother instantly sent one of our servants
with such a threat of vengeance if they did not
immediately desist, that the child was at once re-
leased, and quiet was restored to our house, but
not tranquillity to our minds. This same wretched
woman periodically laments the loss of her son,
the father of this child, and fills the air with her
discordant wailings regularly every alternate Mon-
day. She has always been to us a most annoying
neighbour, and is the more so now that we know
the hypocrisy of her lamentations.

The Muslim ceremonies that have reference to
the dead are, however, generally very interesting;
and their wailings would always be deeply affect-
ing, were they always sincere, and not confined to
stated periods; for they seem to express the most
intense, heart-breaking, despairing grief. The art
of wailing in the most approved style appears to be
an accomplishment that can only be acquired by
long practice; and regular professors of it are
usually hired on the occasior of the death of a
person of the middle or higher classes. These accompany their lamentations with a tambourine,
and occasionally interrupt their screams by plaintive

songs. Their performances, and those of the female
mourners in general, are such as were practised in
most remote ages ; such as we see portrayed upon
the walls of the ancient Egyptian tombs, and such
as are mentioned in many parts of the Holy Scrip-
tures ; as in 2 Chron. xxxv. 25 ; Jerem. ix. 18 ;
Amos v. 16 ; and St. Matt. ix. 23 ; vividly bringing to mind " the minstrels and the people making
a noise" for the death of the daughter of Jairus.
As illustrative of the Bible, these and other Eastern
customs are to me most especially interesting.
" Consider ye," says Jeremiah, exhorting his
countrymen to bewail their disobedience, " and
call for the mourning women, that they may come :
and send for the cunning women, that they may
come : and let them make haste, and take up a
wailing for us, that our eyes may run down with
tears, and our eyelids gush out with waters :" and
by the same means the feelings of a mourning
Eastern family seem to be most powerfully excited
in the present day, for, in general, the most piercing
cries and screams that I hear, on account of a
death, are those which interrupt the lamentations
of the hired mourner, who is " cunning" in her
art. The cemeteries in the neighbourhood of Cairo
are among the most picturesque of the various
scenes which surround us ; and in these are many
private burial-grounds, each belonging to one
family, who, if of sufficient wealth, have within

Tomb.

its walls a house of mourning. To this house the females of the family regularly repair at the period of each of the two great annual festivals, as well as on extraordinary ones, to bewail their dead; having previously sent thither such furniture as is necessary for their comfort; and there they remain, on the occasions of the two festivals above mentioned, and immediately after a death, three or more days and nights. Some of the houses of mourning are pretty and cheerful-looking buildings, and enlivened by a few trees and flowers; and I believe that the women often find no small pleasure in visiting them; their life being in general so monotonous. Some women, who have not houses in the burial-ground for their reception, have tents pitched for them when requisite.

Yesterday we spent some hours at the Southern cemetery, which is adjacent to the city, but within the confines of the desert; and were much interested in examining the tombs of the family of Mohammed 'Alee. The tombs in the cemetery exhibit a strange mixture of various tastes and dimensions: some are in perfect repair, substantially and well built; others are of more fragile kinds; though many of the smaller monuments are composed entirely of white marble; but the most picturesque are the most ancient; displaying exquisite taste in their general forms, and more especially in their domes and minarets, and their

arabesque decorations; these are of yellow limestone, here and there relieved by columns of white
marble.   The building containing the tombs of the
Páshá's family is surmounted by several domes,
but is low, and in no respect deserving of much
admiration.   How can I tell you of the cheerful
appearance of the interior?   Two noble saloons
are filled with tombs at nearly equal distances :
these are cased with white marble, and most gor-
geously decorated with gilded and painted carved
work.   The floors are covered with beautiful carpets, and the scene has at once a complete air of
gaiety and comfort.   It has little that can lead the
mind to the reflection that this is the resting-place
of the dead.   Such a variety of gay colours, and
such varied forms meet the eye, that if the consciousness intrude that it is a sepulchral building,
it is soon banished by the speculation as to which
tombs may be considered more splendid than those
around them.   We generally gave the preference
to that of the mother of Nezleh Hánum, and of
Mohammad Bey Deftardár: the latter, I think,
bears the palm.

The tombs are generally about eight feet long,
and four high ; and on the top of these is placed
an oblong slab, about a foot thick : the upright
slabs at the head and feet are eight or ten feet
high; and on that at the head is a representation of the head-dress of the deceased, carved in

stone, and painted. There are four unoccupied tombs in the principal saloon, raised, but not decorated. The embellishments altogether are such as only suit saloons appropriated to festivity. Turkish taste is ill calculated for decorating the abodes of the living, and does not apply at all where quiet and solemn effect is indispensable. It is not so with regard to Arabian taste: the Turkish is gaudy and florid: the Arabian is chaste and elegant, as much in domestic architecture as in the construction and decoration of sepulchres and mosques.

I felt that I could at any time spend a day in the saloons above mentioned, admiring the beauties of the place, with much personal comfort, and without the frequent intrusion of any melancholy reflection.

In a charming house, adjoining the tombs, appropriated to the use of the hareem of the keeper, we paid his ladies a visit, and were welcomed with true Eastern hospitality. The chief lady, who was handsomely attired in scarlet cloth, embroidered with gold, is a kind agreeable person, but woefully mistaken in her manner of training the dispositions of children. Two little babies belonging to the hareem were brought in to show us: the eldest, a boy, could just walk; and as soon as he made his appearance, the chief lady called for a stick, that puss, who was quietly crossing the carpet, might

be beaten for his amusement. Not being aware
that the beating was not to be in earnest, I inter-
ceded for the cat; when my acquaintance replied
mysteriously, "I like her very much, I will not
hurt her." Accordingly, she raised her arm with
considerable effort, and let it fall gently. She next
desired one of her slaves to kneel, which the girl
did most gracefully, and bent her head with an air
of mock submission, to receive the kurbáj; and the
same farce was performed. Though neither slave
nor cat was a sufferer on the occasion, the effect
must have been equally bad on the mind of the
child. Alas! for the slaves and cats when he is
big enough to make them feel!

LETTER XXV.

February, 1844.

MY DEAR FRIEND,

ALTHOUGH so many have written of the pyramids, and a new description cannot fail to have something of the character of an often repeated tale, I find much that I must say respecting these stupendous monuments, the greatest, perhaps, of the Wonders of the World, which have been objects of our curiosity and astonishment even in the age of childhood, and the sight of which forms an era in one's life. I will, however, as much as possible, avoid troubling you with a repetition of what you have read, or may read, on this subject, in the works of various travellers.

Having arranged that, during our visit, we should spend our days in a sepulchral grotto, and our nights in a tent, we set out on this agreeable excursion with the most pleasing anticipations. The illusion so general in the East with regard to distance, occasioned by the extraordinary clearness of the atmosphere, is strikingly demonstrated in approaching the pyramids; it is very remarkable that the nearer we approached the objects of our

F 2

destination, the less grand and imposing did they appear. From their aspect, as I first drew near to them, I should have formed a very inadequate idea of their dimensions. As soon as we had crossed the river they appeared within a mile of us; and after we had proceeded more than a league from El-Geezeh, I could scarcely believe that we were still a full league from the pyramids; for the distance to them from El-Geezeh, by the route which we took, is more than six miles, though it is just five miles in a direct line. When we arrived within a mile of the pyramids, the illusion became greater: the courses of stone were then plainly discernible, and it was easy to calculate that they were not more in number than the courses of brick in a house about fifty or sixty feet high. These presented a scale by which the eye was much deceived in estimating the altitude of the structure; being unaccustomed to the sight of stones of such enormous magnitude employed in building. But neither of these causes would be sufficient to produce such an illusion if there were any neighbouring object with which the pyramids might be contrasted. I was fully convinced of this when I arrived at the base of the great pyramid. It was then curious to observe how distant appeared those places where I had thought myself nearly at my journey's end. The clearness of the air would have deceived me then, as before; but I was looking at

The Pyramids.

objects less strange to me; such as palm trees, villages, and the tents of Arabs.

. A conspicuous object as we approached the pyramids was an old ruined causeway, most probably a part of that which was built by Kara-Koosh for the convenience of transporting stones from the pyramids to Cairo, when he constructed the citadel, and third wall of that city; and this portion may have been raised on the ruins of that which Herodotus describes, as the more ancient causeway was raised for the purpose of facilitating the conveyance of stones from the quarries on the eastern side of the Nile to the site of the Great Pyramid, to line the passages of that structure, and perhaps to case its exterior.

When we were at least a mile from our journey's end, I remarked to my brother, " The pyramids do not appear so grand as I expected now we are almost close to them." " Almost close to them !" replied he ; " wait a little, and then tell me what you think." Accordingly we rode on ; the provoking appearance of nearness to the objects of our visit surprising me during our whole approach. At this season it occupies three hours to reach the pyramids from Cairo, and this month, on account of its coolness, is particularly agreeable for such an excursion. A kind friend, Mr. Bonomi, well known for the length of time he has spent in this country, and his extensive acquaintance with its monuments, was staying at the pyramids, and prepared for us a tent, and another comfortable place of abode, an ancient sepulchral grotto in a rock, which latter has served as the foundation of a pyramid, now for the most part destroyed. This excavation we found ample and airy, having three large square apertures, serving us as windows, besides the entrance. Our tent was pitched near it, our carpets spread, and our home in the desert had an air of comfort I had hardly anticipated. There is much that is homeish in carrying one's own carpet: place it where you will, in the boat or in the desert, your eyes rest upon it while thinking, and its familiar patterns afford a sort of welcome. The habit of placing the seggádeh (a small carpet) on the saddle enables an Eastern lady to take it wherever she may wander. When she is disposed to rest, her attendants spread it; and nothing is more refreshing during a desert excursion than to rest upon it, and take a simple meal of bread and fruit, and a draught of delicious Nile water.

As soon as possible after our arrival, we mounted the rock on which the pyramids are built, and there observed the effect I have described with regard to the objects we had passed on our way. From the brightness of their colour, apparently little changed by the thousands of years that have passed since their erection, the pyramids do not appear venerable: there is an appearance of freshness about

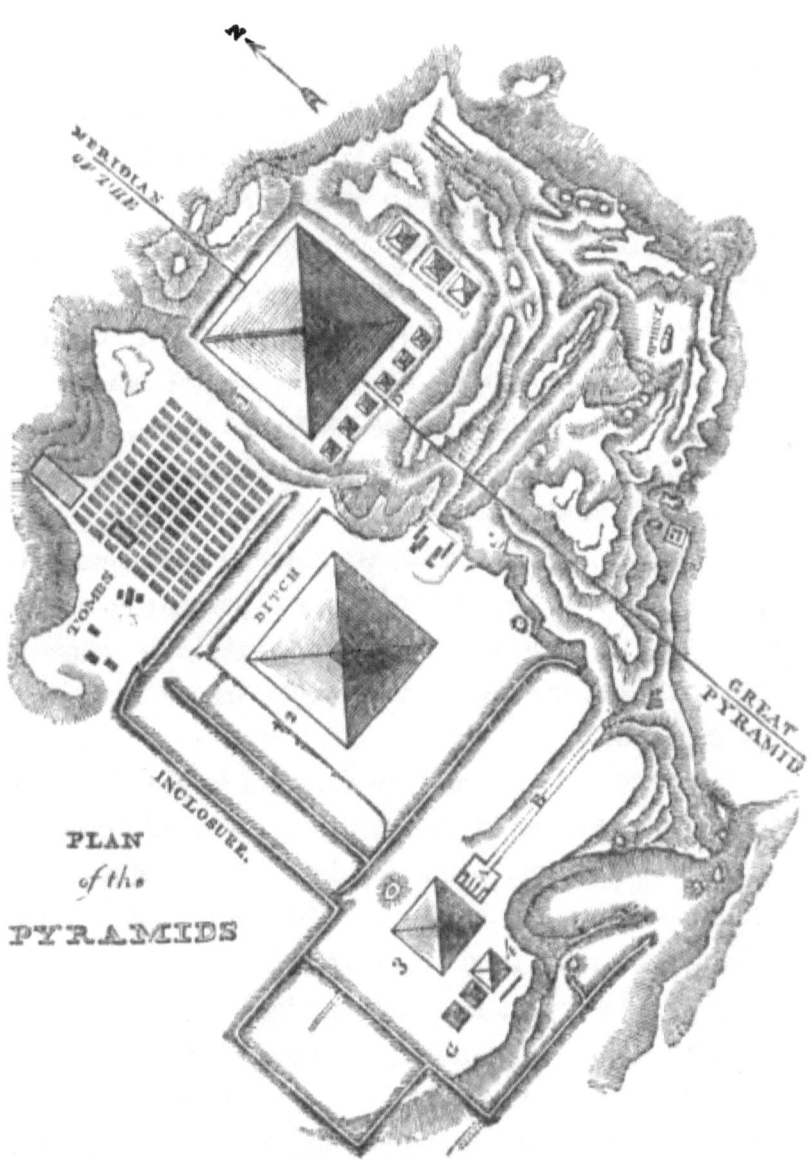

PLAN
of the
PYRAMIDS

A, Remains of an antient building; B, Great causeway: D, Pyramids dilapidated; G, Pyramids with steps; 1, Great pyramid; 2, Second pyramid; 3, Third pyramid; 4, Fourth pyramid.

F 3

them which amazed me : but with regard to their wonderful magnitude, I found that I was no longer disappointed when I had ascended the rocky elevation on which they rest: when I was within a few yards of the base of the Great Pyramid, I was enabled to the full to comprehend its vastness.

We lingered late among the objects of our visit, and were interested in observing the enormous shadows of the two greater pyramids, stretching across the cultivated plain to the river, as the sun was setting. The general view from the rocky eminence on which they are built is the most imposing that can be conceived.

Returning to our grotto, we enjoyed our evening meal with the appetite of desert travellers, and went to rest with our minds impressed by reflections on what we had seen, and by the novelty of our situation.

We were not the only dwellers in tombs during our stay near the pyramids; for a row of sepulchral excavations, which Colonel Vyse and his party occupied in 1837, are now inhabited by a Nubian, who has taken possession of them to afford lodgings (for a small remuneration) to travellers. Also at a short distance from our grotto, an Arab had taken up his abode in a similar but better tomb. Living there as a hermit, he is esteemed a saint by the people of the neighbouring villages, and is supported entirely by casual charity. Very

probably he has adopted the life of an anchorite
because he is idle, and finds it easier to depend on
others than to gain his own bread. It is common
to see the Arabs on their way to leave a deposit of
bread or other food, and sometimes money, with
this recluse, more especially on Friday, when he
receives numerous visitors.

My brother, during a long visit to the pyramids
in 1825, occupied one of the tombs of which the
Nubian has now taken possession. They are excavated in the eastern front of the rocky eminence
on which stands the Great Pyramid. At that time
a family consisting of a little old man (named 'Alee)
his wife (who was not half his equal in age) and a
little daughter, occupied a neighbouring grotto;
guarding some antiquities deposited there by Caviglia. Besides these, my brother had no nearer
neighbours than the inhabitants of a village about
a mile distant. The Sheykh 'Alee made himself
useful in bringing water from a well which Caviglia had dug in the sandy plain, just at the foot of
the slope before the grottoes. He was a poor half-
witted creature, but possessed strong feelings, as
was exemplified by an occurrence which happened
during my brother's stay at the pyramids. One
afternoon, his cook had sent old 'Alee's little girl
to the neighbouring village to purchase some tobacco. The child not having returned by sunset
my brother became uneasy, and dispatched a ser-

vant to search for her, and bring her back. 'Alee had also become anxious, and had sent his wife for the same purpose; but when the night had closed in, and he had received no tidings of the little girl, he became almost frantic: he beat his breast, stamped on the ground, and continued for sometime incessantly screaming, "Yá Mebrookeh! yá Mebrookeh!" (the name of the child, signifying blessed.) After my brother had endeavoured for a little while to pacify him, he set off towards the village. About five minutes more elapsed, and my brother was sitting before the grotto, wondering that no one had returned, and that not even his two Bedawee guards had come as usual, when he was alarmed by loud and piteous cries in the desert plain before him. Leaving a servant in the grotto —for a strange youth was there—my brother ran towards the spot whence the voice seemed to issue. As it was dark, he could see nothing; but after he had proceeded some distance, he heard the following words repeated very rapidly over and over again. "I testify that there is no deity but God, and I testify that Mohammad is God's apostle;"— and soon he found poor old 'Alee lying on the ground. He told my brother that an 'efreet (or demon) had seized him by the throat, and thrown sand into his mouth, and that he was almost suffocated. (It seems that the Arabs are subject to a spasm in the throat, which they attribute to the

above cause.) The two Bedawees, in the meantime, whom the servant and 'Alee's wife had engaged to assist them in their search, had found the
child, and were, like my brother, drawn to that
spot by the old man's cries. They helped him to
walk back, but the poor creature had been so ter-
rified and distressed, that for several days after he
was quite idiotic.

· On the second day after my brother had taken
up his quarters at the pyramids, a young Bedawee
—the stranger I have mentioned—claimed from
him the rights of hospitality. He remained with
him until he quitted his sepulchral abode, and,
being a very clever and witty youth, amused him
exceedingly, every evening while he was smoking
his pipe, by reciting stories and verses from the
popular romance of 'Aboo-Zeyd : but at the same
time he gave much offence to my brother's Egyptian servants, by his contempt of the felláheen (or
peasants). He had deserted from the Páshá's army
of regular troops, as he frankly confessed; and
was afraid to enter the villages, lest he should be
recognized, and sent to the camp. When my
brother was leaving the pyramids, he asked this
young man what he would now do for provision,
as he dared not enter the villages. He replied,
" Who brought *you* here? God is bountiful."

On the occasion of our visit to the pyramids, my
brother inquired of our guards if they knew or

remembered poor old 'Alee, to which one of them
replied that he was his son, and that he had been
dead for some years. He then inquired whether
Mebrookeh was living—" Yes," answered the man,
" she is well and married, and the mother of two
children." He went on to assure my brother he
remembered his former visits well, and there was
something satisfactory in the prospect of being
guarded by one man, at least, who, for old acquaintance sake, might be on the alert. This man,
though especially remarkable for his honesty, is
not distinguished for his social virtues—he has
married ten wives, and says he would marry twenty
if he could afford to do so ; asserting that although
he has divorced several, he has only done so because they deserved it, for that they failed in their
duty to him, notwithstanding his kindness to them.
According to his own account, he was always good
to them ; he never reviled, but *only* beat them !
The facility of divorce is a prodigious evil; often
productive of want and misery. It is sadly common to find wives rejected for some trifling offence ;
when a kind admonition would have shown them
all that had been amiss in their conduct, and would
have rendered them valuable helpmates. I grieve
to say that wives here are generally divorced merely
from caprice.

Our guards, three in number, were remarkably
picturesque objects ; more like Bedawees than like

peasants; belonging to a tribe which, not many
years ago, exchanged the life of desert-wanderers
for that of agriculturists; and having retained the
dress of their fathers, which consists chiefly of a
loose shirt, and a kind of blanket, which envelops
the body, and gives to the wearer an appearance
quite primeval. It was at first amusing, but at last
very tiresome, to hear these men calling to each
other during the whole night, as though they feared
their companions might be asleep: their constant
repetition of, " Open your eyes! open your eyes
well!" effectually kept us watching also. One
guard lay outside the tent, close to my head, and
amused himself by singing constantly. I should
have been very happy if something more substantial
than canvass had separated me from such a lively
neighbour. We rose in the morning fatigued, but
the invigorating desert-air soon revived us; and
we set out on our adventures with becoming
energy.

The bed of rock on which the Great Pyramid is
situated is about one hundred and fifty feet above
the sandy plain which intervenes between it and the
cultivated land. It is a soft testaceous lime-stone,
abounding particularly with those little petrifactions described by Strabo as found in great quan-
tities around the pyramids, and supposed to be
petrified lentils, the leavings of the workmen who
built the pyramids! These abound in many parts

of the chain of mountains by which the valley of
the Nile is confined on this side. The stone, when
newly cut, is of a whitish colour; but, by exposure
to the air, it becomes darker, and assumes a yellowish tint. The level parts and slopes of the rock
are covered with sand and pebbles and fragments
of stone, among which are found pieces of granite
and porphyry, rock crystal, agates, and abundance
of petrified shells, &c.

The Great Pyramid is that which is described
by Herodotus as the work of a Pharaoh named
Cheops, whom Diodorus Siculus calls Chem-
mis. Diodorus adds, that some attributed this
pyramid to a king named Armæus. According to
Manetho (a better authority in that case), it was
founded by Suphis, the second king of the Fourth
Dynasty, which was the second dynasty of the
Memphite kings.

Colonel Vyse's most interesting discoveries of
the hieroglyphic names of the royal founders of the
first and third pyramids afford remarkable confirma-
tions of the truth of the statements of Manetho and
others respecting these monuments. The name of
the founder of the Great Pyramid in hieroglyphics,
according to the pronunciation of different dialects
is Shofo, or Khofo: the former nearly agreeing
with the Suphis of Manetho, the latter with the
Cheops of Herodotus.

The height of the Great Pyramid is not much

greater than that of the second: the former having lost several ranges at the top; while the upper part of the latter is nearly entire: but the base of the former is considerably larger; though the difference is not very remarkable to the eye, and in the solidity and regularity of its construction, it is vastly superior.

The pleasure which is felt by the modern traveller in surveying the pyramids is not a little increased by the consideration of their venerable antiquity, and the reflection that many philosophers and heroes of ancient times have in like manner stood before them, wrapt in admiration and amazement. The stupendous magnitude of the Great Pyramid is most clearly apparent when the observer places himself near one of its angles. The view of the pyramid from this point, though the best that can be obtained, cannot convey an adequate idea of its size; for a gap in the angle, which appears to be near the summit, is not much more than half-way up. Thus greatly is the eye deceived by this extraordinary object.

Each side of the base of the Great Pyramid is seven hundred and thirty-three feet square, and the perpendicular height is four hundred and fifty-six feet, according to my brother's measurement. It consists of two hundred and three courses, or layers of stone; therefore the average height of a single

course is about two feet and a quarter : but the
courses vary in height. from about *four* feet to *one*
foot. The lower courses are higher than the rest ;
and the lowest is hewn out of the solid rock ; as is
also part of the second. Opposite the angle from
which my brother's view was taken, about twelve
feet distant, is a square place, twelve feet in width,
and between two and three inches in depth ; apparently marking the place of the original corner-
stone of the pyramid. About the middle of each
side of the pyramid, the exterior stones have been
much broken by the masses which have been rolled
down from above ; but at the angles they are more
entire, and *there*, consequently, the ascent is not
difficult. The upper and lower surfaces of the
stones are smoothly cut ; but the sides have been
left very rough, and in many cases, not square :
the interstices being filled up with a coarse cement,
of a pinkish colour. This cement is, in some parts,
almost as hard as the stone itself ; and sometimes
very difficult to detach. Among the dust and small
fragments of stone which have crumbled away from
the sides and yet rest upon the upper surfaces of
the steps, or exterior stones, we find a great number of the small petrifactions in the form of lentils,
which I have before mentioned.

Dr. Lipsius lately gave, at a meeting of the
Egyptian Society in this city, a very interesting

account of the mode in which the Great Pyramid, and similar monuments, appear to have been constructed, as suggested by Mr. Wild, an English architect, accompanying the Doctor. The following engraving will explain the description of the system which appears to have been adopted :—

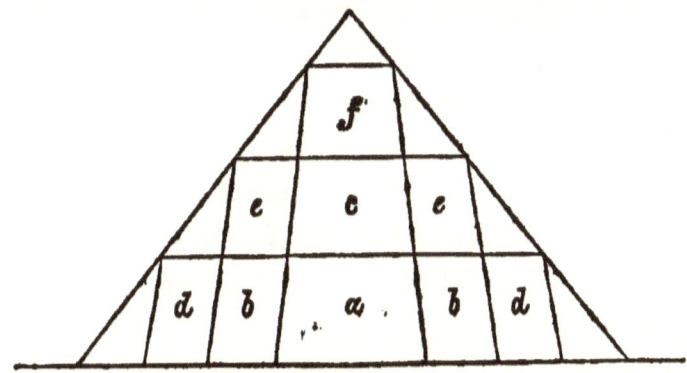

A structure of moderate size, *a*, with its sides slightly inclining inwards, containing, or covering the sepulchral chamber, and with a flat top, was first raised. Then a structure, *bb*, of the same height as the former, with its exterior sides similarly inclined, and its top flat, was raised around. Next, another structure, *c*, was raised on the first. Another circumstructure, *dd*, was raised around that marked *bb* ; then another, *ee*, around the structure *c*, then another structure, *f*, upon the latter. After this manner, the building probably continued to increase (like the royal tombs at Thebes) as long as the founder reigned. The structure was finished, as Herodotus.

says, from the top downwards. A small pyramid
being constructed on the top, occupying the whole
of the highest platform, and the angles formed by
the other platforms, and the sides of the structures
against which they were built being filled up, the
simple pyramidal form was made out. The several
platforms composed convenient ample stages on
which to raise the massive stones employed in the
construction. This mode of construction was certainly practised in some of the pyramids, and most
probably in all, excepting those of very small
dimensions. That the Great Pyramid and others
originally presented plane sides has been proved by
Colonel Vyse.

On each side of the Great Pyramid is an accu-
mulation of fragments of stone and mortar which
have fallen down from the summit and sides of the
building, and have composed a very compact mass,
which rises, in the centre, to about fifty feet above
the base. The sand of the desert has contributed
but little to augment these slopes of rubbish, which
are nearly of the same height on each side of the
pyramid. That on the northern side forms a convenient acclivity to the entrance.

The ascent to the summit of the Great Pyramid
is not dangerous, though rather tedious, as the
description of the exterior must have shown. At,
or near, any of the angles, there is, on almost

every course, or range of stones, a secure and
wide footing; but some of the steps are breast-
high; and these, of course, are awkward masses
to climb. I had fully determined to attempt
the ascent; but the wind was so high during
the period of our visit, that I dared not do so.
On some other occasion I hope to be more fortunate.

Many stones have been thrown down from the
top of the Great Pyramid, which consequently
wants about twenty-five feet (or perhaps something more) of its original height; for, without
doubt, it terminated in a point. It appears, therefore, that its original height was, at the least, four
hundred and eighty feet. It is worthy of remark
that Diodorus Siculus describes the top of the
pyramid as being six cubits (or nine feet) square;
Pliny states it to have been, in his time, twenty-
five feet; or, according to some copies of his work,
fifteen feet; the latter of which readings must be
considered the more correct. Several courses of
stone have been thrown down in later ages; so
that now, on arriving at the summit, there is a
platform thirty-three feet square, upon which, near
the eastern edge, are a few stones yet remaining of
two upper courses. Upon these the names of many
travellers are cut. The platform is quite flat; the
stones being well joined and cemented. The ascent

to the summit generally occupies between fifteen
and twenty minutes.

The view from the summit of the Great Pyramid
is described by my brother as being of a most extraordinary nature. On the eastern side the eye
ranges over an extensive verdant plain, watered by
numerous canals, and interspersed with villages
erected upon mounds of rubbish, and surrounded
by palm-trees. In the distance is the Nile; beyond
which are seen the lofty minarets and citadel of
Cairo, backed by the low yellow range of Mount
Mukattam. Turning towards the opposite side,
the traveller beholds a scene exactly the reverse:
instead of palm-groves and corn-fields, he sees
only the undulating sandy hills of the great Syrian
Desert. The view of the second pyramid, from
this commanding situation, is extremely grand.
A small portion of the third pyramid is also seen;
with one of the small pyramids on its southern
side. The space which lies on the west of the
Great Pyramid, and north of the second, is covered
with oblong tombs, having the form of truncated
pyramids; which from that height appear like
patches of gravel. The head of the Great Sphinx,
and the distant pyramids of Aboo-Seer, Sakkárah,
and Dahshoor, are seen towards the south-south-
east.

About half an hour or more after sunset, the

gloom contributed much to the grandeur and so-
lemnity of the scene. On one occasion my brother
ascended the Great Pyramid about two hours before
daybreak, and waited upon the summit until sun-
rise. He found it extremely cold, and the wind,
sweeping up the northern side of the pyramid,
sounded like a distant cataract. The second pyramid was, at first faintly discernible, appearing of
vastly more than even real magnitude. Soon after,
its eastern side was lighted up by the rising moon ;
and the effect was truly sublime.

On the second day after he had taken up his
quarters at the pyramids, during the visit to which
I have referred, he went out without his pistols ;
and in the evening one of his guards reproved him
for having done so. "How easy," he observed,
" would it be for one of our people (the Bedawees)
to rob you, and, if you resisted, to murder you,
and throw you down one of the mummy-pits, and
who would ever know what was become of you ?"
On the following day he ascended the Great Pyramid alone, but not unarmed. While on the summit,
he perceived a solitary Arab, making towards the
pyramid, from the west. He began to ascend the
south-western angle, and when he arrived about
half-way up, little thinking that my brother's tele-
scope was directed towards him, he stopped, and
took out a pistol from a case which was slung by

his side, looked at it, and then continued the ascent.
As it was evident that the fellow had no good inten-
tions, my brother called to him, and desired him to
descend ; but he either did not hear him, or would
not obey.   My brother then discharged a pistol, to
show him that he was not without the means of
defence.   Upon this, he immediately began to
return, and, having reached the base, walked
slowly away into the desert.

Under the present government, travellers seldom
are subjected to any danger from the natives in this
or any other part of Egypt ; but from the crowding
and importunity of the Arab guides at the pyramids
they generally suffer much annoyance.   They are
always attended for a considerable distance, sometimes even from El-Geezeh, by a party of Arabs
who are in the habit of extorting money from the
traveller on the top of the Great Pyramid before
they will suffer him to descend.   A few days ago,
a gentleman of distinction bargained with some of
these men to attend him to the summit of the
Great Pyramid ; and when they had done so, they
claimed the promised payment, saying that they
had fulfilled their engagement.   Being afraid to
descend without their aid, he was compelled to
submit to their exactions, and paid them five dollars.

It is pitiable to observe the haste which most of

the travellers to and from India are obliged to make, if able to visit the pyramids at all : some arrived during our stay, ran up the Great Pyramid, descended as rapidly, spent a few minutes within it, and disappeared in a little more than an hour.

———————

LETTER XXVI.

February, 1844.

MY DEAR FRIEND,

THE entrance of the Great Pyramid * is over the sixteenth course, or layer of stone, about fifty feet above the base; a slope of rubbish, as I said before, leading up to it.† It is nearly in the centre, or equidistant from either angle of the northern side of the pyramid: the eye would hardly discover that it is not *exactly* so; though really twenty feet, or rather more, to the eastward of the centre. The opening of the pyramid seems to have been attended with considerable difficulty; a vast number of stones having been torn down above and before the aperture. An inclined plane before the entrance forms an angle of twenty-six degrees and a half with the horizon, being in the same place with the floor of the first passage. The size of the stones above the entrance, and the manner in which they are disposed, are worthy of remark. There is no granite at the entrance of the pyramid; all the blocks are of limestone.

* See *b* in the accompanying section.
† See *a* in the section.

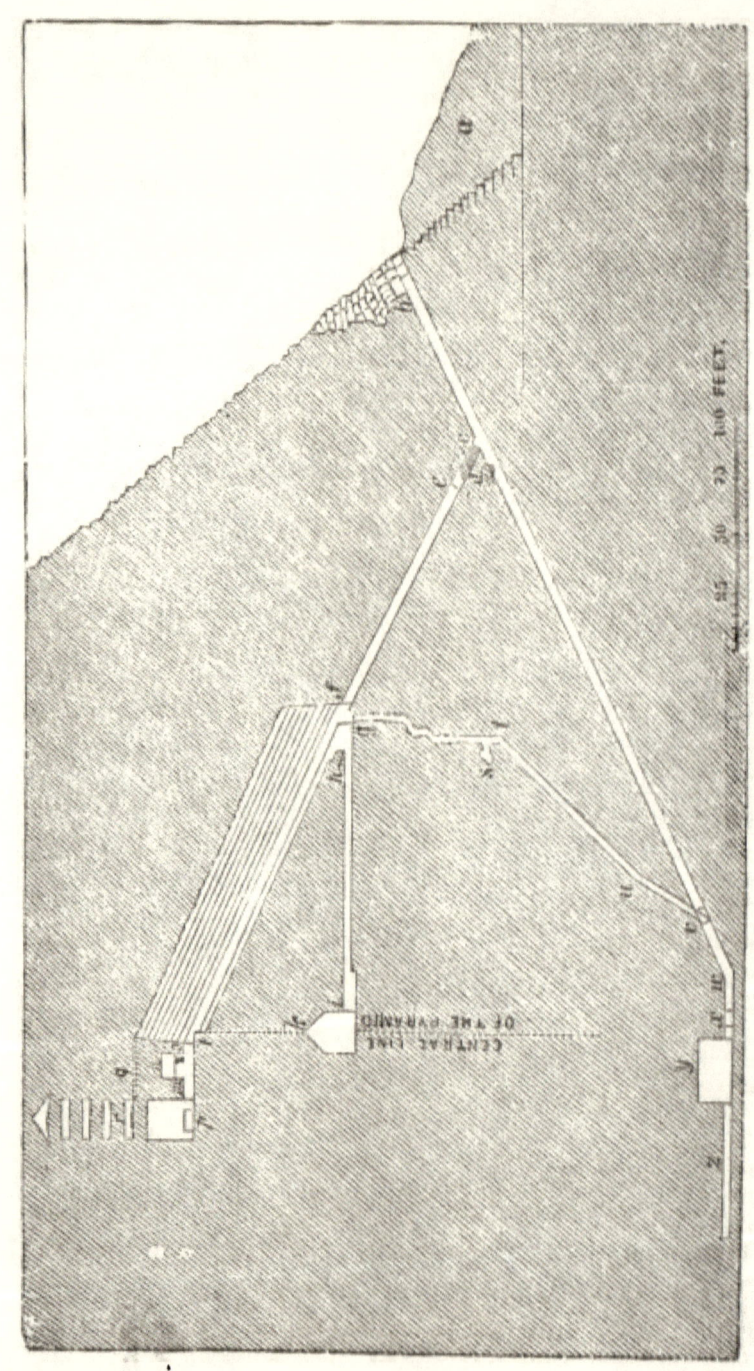

Section of Passages.

Before the traveller enters the pyramid, he should divest himself of some of his clothes (for the heat of the interior is oppressive) and resume them immediately on coming out, to prevent any check of perspiration. The passage by which we enter the Great Pyramid is only four feet high, and three feet six inches (almost exactly two ancient Egyptian cubits) in width, and we are consequently obliged to descend in a crouching position. It is lined above and below and on each side with blocks of limestone,* of a more compact kind than that of which the pyramid is mainly constructed. This superior kind of stone appears to have been brought from the quarries on the eastern side of the Nile, directly opposite the site of Memphis; for stone of the same quality is not found nearer; and Herodotus, and several other ancient writers, inform us that the quarries of the Arabian mountains † supplied materials for the construction of the pyramid. Indeed, they assert that the pyramid was entirely built of stones from these quarries; but this, evidently, was not the case : the stone of which the structure is mainly composed was quarried from

---

* Some travellers, their memories deceiving them, have described this passage as lined with *granite;* others have asserted that it is of *white marble.*

† The mountains on the east of the Nile are so called by ancient Greek and Roman writers, and those on the west the " Lybian Mountains."

the rock in its neighbourhood. The nicety with which the stones are united in the sides of the first passage is very remarkable. In some parts the joint cannot be discerned without a close and minute examination. In the flooring of this passage, and of all the sloping passages in this pyramid, notches have been roughly cut, like steps, to prevent the feet from slipping; but I found them very far from producing the desired effect, being now polished by the naked feet of the guides. These notches have been the work of modern explorers. At the distance of nearly seventy feet (measuring from the outer surface of the huge block above the entrance) we find that one of the stones which form the roofing of the passage has been hewn away precisely at the point where the second passage branches off in an ascending direction (see the letter c in the section). Here we discover the square end of a granite block, which closes the entrance of the second passage, being exactly fitted to fill up the aperture. The persons who opened the pyramid, being unable to remove this obstacle, have made a forced communication with the ascending passage. At the distance of eighty feet (from the entrance of the pyramid) is the forced aperture, on the right side of the passage (see d in the section). It has been made by hollowing out the roofing, and cutting away the upper rt of the side of the lower passage.

· Here the explorer must light his candle (if he
have not done so before), and having ascended
through this opening, finds himself in a large place,
which appears like a natural cavern in a rock.
We now see the upper end of the granite block
before mentioned, or of a second block. Above it
is another, of which a part has been broken off.
Above this the passage (e.f) is seen clear of other
incumbrances, running upwards, but in the same
southern course as the first, or descending passage.
It is of the same dimensions as the first, and has
the same inclination; but its sides and roofing are
very rough, and consequently it has the appearance
of having been cut through solid rock, which is not
really the case. It is a hundred and nine feet long
(measuring from the southernmost of the granite
blocks above mentioned), and the flooring projects
a foot and a half in the same direction. The ascent
of this passage is rather fatiguing. On emerging
from it, we find ourselves at the foot of the Grand
Passage (see f m in the section).

This great passage, ascending to the principal
chamber, is, in comparison with those which lead
to it, wide and lofty. Its length being great, and
its sides and every part of it blackened, as if by
smoke, the further extremity was invisible to us as
we stood at the lower end; and its whole appearance singularly imposing. On our right, as we
stood here, we observed the entrance, or mouth, of

what has been called " the well " (*g*). There we
also, at the lower end of the Grand Passage, remarked some Arabic inscriptions, rudely cut with
a chisel. These, I believe, were first noticed by
Sir Gardiner Wilkinson. My brother read them
to me thus—" Ezbek and Beybars have been here."
" Beybars and Kalaoon El-Elfee have been here."
" Sultán Mohammad. . . . Sa'eed." These three
persons were Memlook sultáns of Egypt, who
reigned in the latter half of the thirteenth century,
at which period, it appears, the Great Pyramid
was open ; if these inscriptions be genuine, which
my brother is a little inclined to doubt.

Under the grand, ascending passage, runs another,
which is horizontal, low, and narrow. The entrance
of the latter (*h*) is fifteen feet three inches from the
projection of a foot and a half before mentioned.
This passage is three feet eleven inches high, and
three feet five inches wide. I found almost as
much difficulty in proceeding here as I had in
ascending and descending the sloping passages ; the
dust and the heat together being here especially
oppressive. It continues of the same dimensions
to the distance of ninety-three feet. Here we find
a descent of one foot eight inches in the floor ; so
that the remainder of the passage is nearly high
enough for a person of middling stature to walk
along it without bending down the head. At the
distance of a hundred and ten feet nine inches (from

its entrance) it terminates (see *i* in the section) at the eastern corner of the north side of a chamber, which is nineteen feet long, and seventeen feet broad (see *k*). This has been called by some travellers the " Queen's Chamber;" from the supposition that the queen of the founder of the pyramid was buried in it. The roof is formed of long blocks of stone, leaning against each other. The height of the chamber, to the commencement of the roof, is thirteen feet and a half; and to the summit, about seven feet more. The floor, sides, and roof are constructed of the same kind of limestone as the passages. In the eastern end (not in the middle, but rather to the right) is a high and narrow recess, five feet wide at the bottom, but becoming narrower towards the top, like the sides of the Grand Passage. It is three feet five inches deep. Within it, four feet from the floor, is the entrance of a forced passage, four feet wide. At the commencement it is square, and smoothly cut; but further on it becomes irregular; and at the distance of fifty feet it terminates at a hollow space, wider and more irregular than the rest. In this chamber and forced passage there is little to detain us. We return to the Grand Passage.

Above the entrance of the horizontal passage which leads to the chamber above described, is a perpendicular (marked *h* in the section). This perpendicular, together with the height of the said passage, is seven feet three inches. The flooring then ascends in the same direction as the other ascending passage; at an angle of twenty-six degrees and a half. At the distance of three feet five inches is another perpendicular or step of only eight inches, above which the floor has the same inclination again; and notches have been cut in it, to facilitate the ascent, which is not easily performed unless without shoes. There is a bench of stone on each side all along the passage, and in the tops of these benches are oblong holes at short intervals: their use is unknown. The width of the passage (including the benches, which are one foot eight inches and a half square), is six feet ten inches; about four ancient Egyptian cubits. The sides of the passage are composed of nine courses of stone from the benches upwards. The stone is of the same kind as that of which the lower passages are constructed. Some travellers have supposed it to be *white marble*, but no marble is found in any part of the pyramid. The two lower courses are even with each other; but each course above projects three inches beyond that below it; and so does each corresponding course at the upper and lower ends of the passage. The length of the whole passage is a hundred and fifty-eight feet. At the distance of five feet and one inch before we reach the upper end, we ascend another perpendicular of two feet eleven inches. The floor beyond is horizontal, forming a small platform (see *l* in the section). From this commences a horizontal passage three feet seven inches and a half in height, and three feet five inches and a half in width (see *m*). Within it, on the right, is the entrance of a *forced* passage, made in search for other chambers than those already known. At the distance of four feet five inches (from the entrance of the *true passage*), commences an open space above (see *n*), the upper part of which is nearly twice as wide as the passage, and nine feet eight inches in length : but the passage below is contracted again to its former height by a kind of portcullis, formed of two blocks of granite one above another, each one foot three inches thick ; these have been let down from the space above between two small projections on each side which form a pair of grooves. Beyond this, the passage (which is here of *granite*), is open as before, to the space above, and there are grooves for the reception of three other portcullises of granite, by which the architect thought that he should for ever prevent access to the mysterious chamber which contains the sarcophagus ; but these have been broken and their fragments carried away. The passage beyond (see *o*), is of its former dimensions, and continues so to the distance of eight feet five inches, its whole length, from the top of the Grand Passage, being twenty-two feet and a half. It terminates at the eastern extremity of the north side of the Grand Chamber (see *p* in the section).

The dimensions of the Great Chamber are especially worthy of remark: the length is thirty-four feet four inches and a half; just twenty ancient Egyptian cubits; the width exactly half that measure. The height is about two feet more than the width. It is entirely constructed of red granite. Near the western end is the sarcophagus; which is also of red granite. It is seven feet and a half in length, three and a half in breadth, and the sides are half a foot thick. No hieroglyphics nor sculptures of any kind adorn it either within or without; its sides are perfectly plain and polished, and its form is simply that of an oblong chest, in every way rectangular. Its lid has been carried away, as well as its original contents; and we find in it nothing but dust and small fragments of stone. It has been much injured at one of its corners by a number of travellers, who have broken off pieces to carry away as memorials. When struck with anything hard, or even with the hand, it sounds like a bell. It rests upon a block of granite considerably larger than any of the other blocks of which the floor is composed.

Why was such an enormous mass placed there? The alabaster sarcophagus in the great tomb opened by Belzoni in the valley of Beebán-el-Mulook, at Thebes, closed the entrance of a deep descent of steps, which has never been explored to its termination : the soft and crumbling nature of the rock through which it is cut rendering any attempt to clear it out extremely dangerous.   The enormous mass of granite under the sarcophagus in the Great Pyramid may have been placed there for a similar purpose, or to cover the mouth of a vault or pit ; so that, in case any violater of the sacred edifice should succeed (notwithstanding the portcullises of granite), in effecting an entrance into the Great Chamber, he might, on discovering the sarcophagus, believe the object of his search to be accomplished. An excavation has been made (I believe by Col. Howard Vyse), beneath this huge stone, but it seems hardly to have been carried sufficiently far. The sides of the chamber are formed of six regular courses of granite blocks, which are united with the greatest exactness, and their surfaces are perfectly even and polished, without hieroglyphics or any other inscriptions or ornaments.   In the northern side near the corner of the entrance is a small aperture, and opposite to it in the southern side is another.   Col. Vyse discovered the termination of each of these, in the exterior of the pyramid : they seem to have been designed for the purpose of ventilation.   The roof of the chamber consists of nine long granite blocks which extend from side to side. The half only of the stone at each end is seen, the other half resting on the wall.

Returning from this chamber we stop at the platform at the upper end of the Grand Passage (see *l* in in the section).* Here we observe at the top of the eastern wall (that is on the left of a person facing the end of the passage), at the height of twenty-four feet, a square aperture which is the entrance of another passage (*q*). Small notches have been cut at the corner all the way up, for the reception of the ends of short pieces of wood, which were thus placed one above another so as to form a kind of ladder. These have been taken away, and the ascent without them is difficult and dangerous. When my brother was here alone some years ago, two Arabs contrived to climb up by means of the little notches, and took with them a strong rope, the end of which he tied round him, and so they drew him up to the top. As soon as he was freed from the rope they demanded of him a present, threatening that if he refused they would descend and leave him there. Though my brother laughed at their threats, they would not for some minutes confess that they were joking. The passage in which he found himself is only two feet four inches square. It turns immediately to the right, and to the distance of a few feet it continues square and of the same dimensions as before, but

---

* There is a remarkable echo in this passage, on account of which it is a custom of travellers to fire a pistol or gun here.

much clogged with dirt; afterwards it becomes
irregular both in direction and in the construction
of its sides, and it was difficult for my brother to
drag himself along it, while numbers of bats
escaped from within and flew against his face. At
the distance of twenty-four feet the passage terminates at the north-east corner of a large but
low place (r). This chamber (if such it may be
called) was discovered by Mr. Davison, who was
British Consul at Algiers, and who visited Egypt
with Mr. Wortley Montague in 1763 and 4, and it
is called by the discoverer's name. It is directly
above the Grand Chamber, and is of the same
width as that chamber, but four feet longer.
The long granite blocks which compose the roof
of the lower chamber form the floor of this, and
the first and last of these blocks are here seen
entire. The upper surface of each of them is very
rough, and they are not all of the same thickness.
The roof also of this place is formed of long blocks
of granite eight in number. The height is scarcely
more than three feet. In the south-east corner is
a small forced passage which ascends a few feet.
The second roof above the Grand Chamber was
made to secure the lower roof, which otherwise
might have been broken down by the superin-
cumbent masses. Col. Vyse discovered over
Davison's chamber three others similar to it one
above another, and above the uppermost of these

another with a pointed roof; and in making this discovery he made one of much greater importance, that of two hieroglyphic names, rudely inscribed as quarry-marks; one of them certainly the name of the founder, as before mentioned; the other, according to some, a variation of the same name; according to others, the name of a predecessor or successor of the founder.

I scarcely need tell you that I did not descend what is called the well. It was explored by Mr. Davison, and afterwards in 1801 by Col. Coutelle; but its termination and use remained involved in uncertainty and mystery, until it was cleared out in 1817 by Caviglia. On the right of the lower end of the Grand Passage two feet below the floor, are three low steps occupying a space of four feet and a half in length. Beyond them is the mouth of the first shaft which is two feet two inches square. Here are little notches roughly cut in the sides in which to place the fingers and toes, and as the space is narrow, a person *may* descend without the aid of a rope, as my brother did, but he found it difficult and dangerous to do so. The ascent is attended with less danger, and seems precisely like climbing a chimney. At the depth of a few feet it becomes very rugged and irregular, and continues so for nearly fifty feet. After descending rather more than sixty feet, an aperture is seen on the southern side, which is the entrance of a kind of grotto (*s*) between five and six feet high, and about three times as long, turning to the right. It is hollowed out in a vein of coarse but compact gravel, and the well, in consequence of this vein, is lined with masonry for the space of a few feet above and below the grotto. Where the masonry ceases (*t*) the well takes a sloping direction and continues so to the bottom; but towards the bottom (see *u* in the section) the slope becomes more steep. All the sloping part is cut through the solid rock below the foundation of the pyramid, and is of a square form. At the bottom of the well (*v*) is a horizontal passage six feet long, communicating with the first passage, two hundred and twelve feet below the aperture by which one ascends to the second passage.

The first passage of the pyramid from the aperture last mentioned, continues in the same direction, and is of the same dimensions, but is cut through the solid rock, and is not lined with masonry. The aperture which communicates with the bottom of the well is two feet ten inches broad. It is on the right of a person descending the first passage. This passage continues in the same direction to the distance of twenty-three feet further (see *w* in the section), beyond which it is horizontal, and so low and incumbered with rubbish, that the explorer is obliged to drag himself along in a prostrate position. At the distance of sixteen feet nine inches

there is a recess (x) on the right side three feet
four inches deep, and six feet five inches wide.
Four feet and a half beyond this, the passage terminates at the eastern extremity of the north side
of a large excavated chamber (y).

The Great Excavated Chamber is nearly under
the centre of the pyramid. It is twenty-seven feet
broad, and sixty-six feet long. The roof is flat,
but the floor is very uneven. At the entrance the
chamber is fifteen feet high; towards the western
end the rock rises perpendicularly half-way towards
the ceiling, and there are masses of strange forms,
but not altogether irregular, rising still higher,
and nearly touching the top of the chamber. In
the floor at the lower end is a wide hollow space
nearly filled with rats' dung. Immediately opposite
the entrance is a level passage (z), low and narrow,
running towards the south; it terminates abruptly
at the distance of fifty-five feet. The floor of the
chamber is just a hundred feet below the level of
the external base of the pyramid. It appeared
evident to my brother that this great chamber was
an unfinished excavation. Mr. Salt thought otherwise: "He had flattered himself that it would
turn out to be that described by Herodotus as containing the tomb of Cheops, which was insulated by
a canal from the Nile; but the want of an inlet, and
its elevation of thirty feet above the level of the
Nile at its highest point, put an end to this delusive

idea." This great chamber was discovered by Caviglia, of whose operations in the Great Pyramid, and in the neighbouring tombs, an interesting account is given in the 19th vol. of the 'Quarterly Review.' After having explored the well, and endeavoured, in vain, to draw up the rubbish with which the lower end was filled, he turned his attention to the clearing of the first passage of the pyramid, which, until that time, had been supposed to terminate just below the aperture which communicates with the second passage. In the prosecution of this work (which was one of much difficulty, as the passage was choked with large fragments of stone), he discovered the communication with the bottom of the well, and, continuing his operations, soon after entered the Great Excavated Chamber.

Such is the description of all that is now known of the interior of the Great Pyramid. It has been calculated that there might be within this stupendous fabric, three thousand seven hundred chambers, each equal in size to the Sarcophagus Chamber, allowing the contents of an equal number of such chambers to be solid, by way of separation.* Yet this enormous pile seems to have been raised merely as a sepulchral monument, to contain, perhaps, one single mummy, not a particle of which now remains in the place in which it was deposited with

* Quarterly Review—vol. 19, page 401.

so much precaution ;* unless there be yet undis-
covered any other receptacle for the royal corpse
than the sarcophagus in the Granite Chamber.
Herodotus and Diodorus Siculus assert that the
building of the Great Pyramid occupied about
twenty years, and according to the former, a hundred thousand men—according to the latter three
hundred and sixty thousand men—were employed
in its construction.

The Great Pyramid is surrounded, on three sides,
by almost innumerable tombs. On the east are
three small pyramids; and on the same side, and
on the west and south, are many oblong tombs,
flat-topped, and with sides inclining inwards. Some
persons who have been unreasonable enough to
doubt whether the pyramids are sepulchral monuments, must, I think, be convinced of their error
by the discoveries of Colonel Vyse: long before
which, my brother found bones and mummy-rags
in the principal pyramid of Sakkárah.

* Most ancient authors who have described this monument assert, in opposition to Diodorus, that its founder was
buried in it.

LETTER XXVII.

February, 1844.

MY DEAR FRIEND,

I FEAR that I might weary you if I gave you a description of the other pyramids as full as that of the first; and, as they are far less interesting, I would pass them over entirely; but a few remarks respecting them, some of which I owe to my brother, I do not refrain from offering, as I think they will interest you. It is no trifle, I assure you, for a woman to explore the interior of the Great Pyramid. My mind continued so impressed with the difficulties of this undertaking, for some time, that I could not forget them, even in my dreams. The examination of the others is somewhat less arduous.

The name of the founder of the Second Pyramid, commonly called that of Chephrenes, still remains involved in some degree of doubt. But in some of the tombs in the neighbourhood, we find a king's name, in hieroglyphics, which, according to different dialects, may be read Khephré or Shefré; and it seems highly probable that the king to whom

this name belongs was the builder of the pyramid
in question.

This pyramid is but little inferior in magnitude
to the first. From some points of view, it even
appears more lofty, as it stands on ground about
thirty feet higher than that on which the first rests,
and its summit is almost entire. A large portion
of its smooth casing remains on the upper part,
forming a cap which extends from the top to about
a quarter of the distance thence to the base. Notwithstanding this, Arabs often ascend to its summit; and many European travellers have done the
same. In its general construction, this pyramid
is inferior to the first; and its interior is less remarkable. By a sloping passage, similar to the
first in the Great Pyramid, but cased with granite,
and then by a long horizontal passage hewn through
the rock, broken by two perpendicular descents,
and sloping ascents, we reach the Great Chamber.
This is similar in form to the " Queen's Chamber"
in the Great Pyramid, and contains a plain sarcophagus of granite, among blocks of the same material
lately torn up from the floor, in which the sarcophagus was embedded. :

Several Arabic inscriptions are scrawled with
charcoal upon various parts of this chamber. Most
of these were written before the opening of the
pyramid by Belzoni, and are nearly illegible; generally recording the visits of Arabs, and in the

modern Arabic characters. My brother could not find any date among them. From his manuscript notes, I copy the following observations respecting one of these inscriptions which has excited especial attention : consisting of two lines, written in the same characters as the rest, and with the same material, but not so imperfectly legible. " Belzoni particularly remarked these two lines, and took a Copt scribe to copy them ; but this man did not faithfully execute his task : he concluded that the second line was a continuation of the first, which is far from being certain, and gave a transcript in which he presumed to restore what was defective in the original. His transcript has been thus translated by Mr. Salame : ' The Master Mohammed Ahmed, lapicide, has opened them ; and the Master Othman attended this (opening) ; and the King Alij Mohammed at first (from the beginning) to the closing up.' This inscription has exceedingly puzzled the learned Orientalists of Europe ; and great pains have been taken to find out who was the king mentioned in it, and at what period he reigned. It unfortunately happens that the first line is almost wholly defaced ; a traveller having scribbled his name over it : the two first words, however, have not been written over ; and I must pronounce it very uncertain whether they are as in the transcript above-mentioned, and consequently, whether the inscription contain any mention of the ' open-

ing' of the pyramid. But the second line, which
is the more important, has not been defaced like
the first; and the greater part of it is so plain that
it can hardly be read otherwise than thus: ' El-
Khaleel 'Alee, the son of Mohammad . . . ,
has been here;' or, in the order of the Arabic
words, ' Has been here El-Khaleel 'Alee, the son
of Mohammad . . .' It is quite evident that
the word which Belzoni's copyist makes ' el-melik,'
or ' the King,' is a proper name. Another inaccu-
racy in the copy published by Belzoni is the omission
of the word signifying ' son,' after ' 'Alee.' Thus
we find that this inscription (instead of recording
the visit of a king, or perhaps, even alluding to the
opening of the pyramid) is probably nothing more
than the Arabic scrawls which are seen in great
numbers on many of the monuments of Egypt. It,
and others similar to it, are of some interest, however, as showing that the pyramid was open at a
comparatively late period."

The third pyramid, commonly attributed to My-
cerinus, or Mencheres, was opened by Colonel
Vyse, who found in it the mummy-case of its
founder, bearing the hieroglyphic name of Men-
karé. This pyramid, though small in comparison
with the first and second, its base being about three
hundred and thirty feet, and its perpendicular
height about two hundred, is a very noble monument. Its construction is excellent; and it was

distinguished by being partly, or wholly, cased
with granite. Several courses of the granite casing-
stones remain at the lower part. The chamber in
which the sarcophagus was found, and the entrance-
passage, are formed of granite ; and the roof of the
former is composed of blocks leaning together, and
cut so as to form an arched ceiling. The sarcophagus was lost at sea, on its way to England.
The third pyramid was the first that I entered ;
and highly was I gratified by the view of its interior, after I had summoned courage to crawl
through its entrance, which was almost closed by
huge masses of stone.

Adjacent to the pyramids which I have mentioned
are several others ; but these are comparatively
insignificant ; and I shall not attempt to describe
them : nor shall I undertake to give you a detailed
account of any of the numerous tombs to which I
have before alluded. Most of these lie in a large
space to the west of the Great Pyramid, and north
of the second ; and are, with few exceptions, disposed in regular lines, from north to south, and
from east to west ; their walls, like the sides of the
pyramids, facing the four cardinal points. Some
of them are nearly buried in the drifted sand ; and
many are almost entirely demolished. Some contain no chambers above ground ; but have a pit,
entered from the roof, descending to a sepulchral
chamber. Others contain narrow chambers within

their walls, adorned with painted sculptures in low relief, representing agricultural and other scenes. Most of these are of the same age as the Great Pyramid. In one of them, which is of that age, are represented persons engaged in various arts, carpenters, makers of papyrus-boats (probably like the ark in which Moses was exposed), agricultural employments, the wine-press, eating, dancing, &c. Among the subjects in this tomb, we find two men sitting at a tray which is supported by a low pedestal, and loaded with food : one is holding a fowl in his left hand ; and, with his right, tearing off one of the wings : the other is holding a joint, and about to bite off a piece. Each of these persons is almost naked : had they more clothing, they would exhibit a true representation of two modern Egyptians at their dinner or supper. There are also many sepulchral grottoes, excavated in the rock, in the neighbourhood of the pyramids. In one we find representations of the flocks and herds of the principal occupant, with the number of each kind : he had 835 oxen, 220 cows with their young, 2234 he-goats, 760 asses, and 974 rams. This interesting tomb is of the remote age of Khephré, or Shefre, before-mentioned. It is in the front of the rocky elevation on which the Great Pyramid stands, a little to the right of Colonel Vyse's quarters, facing the valley of the Nile.

Had I attempted a regular description of the pyra-

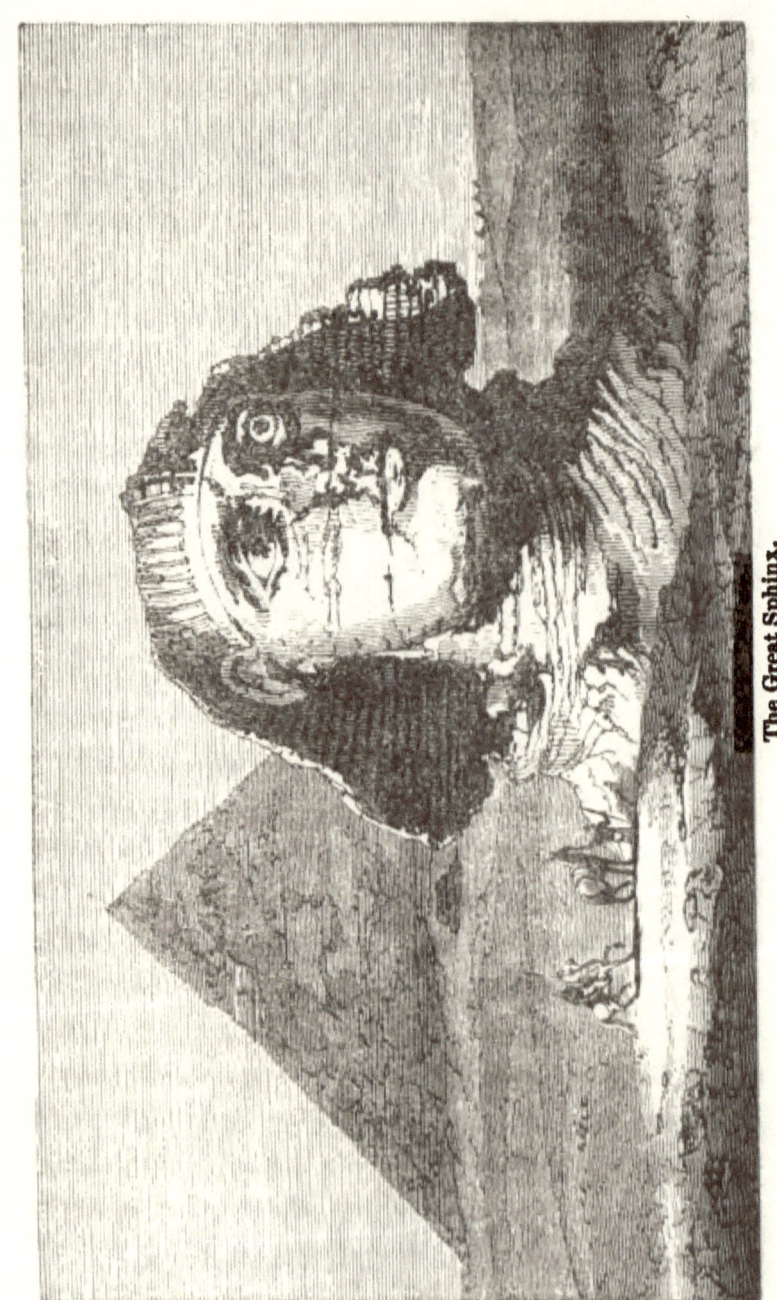

The Great Sphinx.

mids and the monuments around them, I should have
begun with the Great Sphinx, which faces the traveller approaching the Great Pyramid by the easi-
est route from the south-east, and lies but a short
distance from that route. Its huge recumbent
body, and its enormous outstretched fore legs, are
almost entirely buried in sand and rubbish. The
head alone is twenty feet high. The face (which
lays claim to be regarded as a portrait of Thothmes
IV., whom many believe to have reigned during
the bondage of the Israelites in Egypt, or shortly
before or after, and who may have been the very
Pharaoh in whose reign the Exodus took place) is
much mutilated; the nose being broken off. This
loss gives to the expression of the face much of
the negro character : but the features of the countenance of the ancient Egyptian, as well as the com-
parative lightness of complexion, widely distinguished him from the negro ; and the nose of the
former greatly differed from that of the latter.
At first the countenance of the Sphinx, disfigured
as it is, appeared to me absolutely ugly ; but when
I drew near, I observed in it a peculiar sweetness
of expression, and I did not wonder at its having
excited a high degree of admiration in many travellers. The whole of this extraordinary colossus
was doubtless painted : the face still retains much
of its paint, which is red ochre, the colour always
employed by the ancient Egyptians to represent

the complexion of their countrymen ; yellow or
pink being used by them for that of the Egyptian
women.   All that is visible of the Sphinx is hewn
out of a mass of limestone rock, which perhaps
naturally presented something of the form which
art has given to it.

I did not think to have written to you so much
on the pyramids and the monuments around them ;
but having entered upon the subject, I have found
it difficult to stop. So wonderful in themselves
are the principal pyramids, and so impressive by
reason of their remote antiquity, that all other
existing works of man must, I think, in comparison
with them, sink into insignificance.   I could
hardly believe that monuments of such stupendous
magnitude, and such admirable construction, were
erected several centuries before the period of the
Exodus, were it not for the fact that the Tower of
Babel, probably an equally wonderful edifice, was
raised in an age yet earlier.

During this excursion I was gratified by observing among innumerable Arabs belonging to the
villages not a single instance of blindness, a
calamity so common in Cairo.   These peasants
seem to enjoy a very small share of this world's
goods ; but the exhilarating air usually blowing
from the neighbouring desert has an extraordinary
effect on their health and spirits.

On the morning before our departure several

Pyramids and Arabs.

well-dressed young Bedawees arrived near our tent, the sons of the sheykh of a distant village. After dismounting and loitering about for nearly an hour, they confessed to one of our party that they had ridden several miles in the hope of seeing the faces of some European ladies, who, they had been informed, were passing a few days at the pyramids, and they were seriously disappointed on finding veiled ladies only. A few weeks since these same young men enjoyed the treat of seeing an American lady who is travelling in Egypt, and who is a beautiful person. A friend of ours asked their opinion of the lady on that occasion, when they replied that her appearance was "excellent." "But," exclaimed one of the young men, "the sword! the sword! if we dared to use it, we would kill that man," alluding to the lady's companion, "whether her husband, or her brother, and take her ourselves." 'Tis well for pretty women travelling in the East that these lawless Arabs are kept under a degree of subjection by the present government.

LETTER XXVIII.

March, 1844.

MY DEAR FRIEND,

You may have heard of a famous magician in this famous city of Cairo, who, though not supposed to be possessed of art equal to that of Pharaoh's wise men and sorcerers, has perplexed aud confounded several of the most intelligent travellers, by feats very nearly resembling that performed by the Witch of Endor at the request of Saul. Having inscribed a magic square upon the palm of the right hand of any young boy or girl, and poured into the centre of it a little pool of ink, he pretends by means of the repetition of certain invocations to two spirits, and by burning some small strips of paper inscribed with similar invocations, in a chafing-dish containing live coals sprinkled with frankincense and coriander-seed, or other perfume, to make the boy see in this pool of ink the image of any person, living or dead, called for by his employer. My brother has fully described his performances as witnessed by himself and several other travellers more than ten years ago,* the performances of which he was himself witness were not altogether inexplicable, for some of the persons called for were not unknown to fame, and the correct description of others might have been the result of mere guessing; but the facts which he has related on the testimony of others have induced several persons whom I could name to believe them the effects of supernatural agency. The supposed mystery, however, my brother thinks he can now explain, at least so far as to satisfy any reasonable person respecting most, if not all, of the most surprising of the feats to which I have alluded.

A few weeks ago, he was requested by two English travellers, Lord N. and Major G., to witness the performances of this magician, and to act as interpreter on the occasion, in order that they might feel themselves secure from any collusion. But I must give you his own account of the exposure which this request occasioned.

" I was unwilling," he said, " to accede to the proposal made to me, and expressed a reluctance to do so; but I am glad that I at last consented. The magician tried with two boys, and with both of them he utterly failed in every case. His excuse was, that the boys were liars, and described

---

* We reprint this account in the Appendix A, for without this extract from Mr. Lane's work on the ' Modern Egyptians,' his sister's narrative is unintelligible. *Ed.*

the objects which they saw otherwise than as they appeared to them; that the feats were performed not by his own means alone, and that he was not secure from being imposed upon by others. Now if we admit that there is *still* such a thing as real magic, and we know from the Bible such was once the case, we must allow that by occasional failures this man does not show that he is not a true magician, as long as he employs an agent, upon whose veracity and particular qualifications he asserts the success of his performances to depend. Partly, perhaps, from feelings of mortification, and partly with the view of upholding his reputation by urging what he had done on former occasions, he remarked to me that he was successful in the days of 'Osmán Efendee, and that since the death of that person he had been unfortunate.

" This was indeed, for him, a most unfortunate remark. The inference to be drawn from it, that the person whom he named was the main spring of his machinery, was inevitable, more especially when I considered, that in all the instances of his surprising success of which I had heard, this person served as the interpreter; and when I further reflected, that since his death, which took place nearly nine years ago, hundreds of persons had witnessed the performances of this magician, and I had been assured that his successes had been such as could not be said to be even the results of lucky guesses or mere accident, for he had almost always failed. I was at first unwilling to believe that a person whom I always regarded as an honest man, and whom I knew to have been possessed of many excellent qualities, had consented to be a means of imposition; and I remembered that, in the performances which I had myself witnessed, I ascertained that he gave no direction either by word or sign; that he was generally unacquainted in these instances with the personal appearance of the individual called for; that I took care that he should have no previous communication with the boys; and that I had seen the experiment fail when he *could* have given directions to them or to the magician. But the inferences to be derived from these circumstances, in favour of the magician, are surely outweighed by the facts which I have mentioned, resting not only upon the assertions of others, but also upon his own confession. 'Osmán perhaps considered it a light matter to practise such an artifice as that which is thus imputed to him, and perhaps was unwilling to practise it upon me, or feared my detecting him if he attempted to do so. Besides, if many of the performances of the magician had not been far more surprising than those which I witnessed, he would have gained but little notoriety. I satisfied myself that the boy employed in a case which I have mentioned in my work on the

'Modern Egyptians,' was not prompted for the part he played, by my having chosen him from a number of others passing by in the street; and I also felt satisfied that the images which he and another boy professed to have seen, were by some means produced in the ink by the magician, in consequence of their refusal to accept presents which I offered them, with the view of inducing them to confess that they did not really see what they proposed to have seen. As to the former point, I was doubtless right; but as to the latter, I now feel that I was deceived. I believe that the boys saw nothing, and that, having deceived me, they feared to confess the truth. Another difficulty, however, lies in the way of the explanation which I have proposed: two travellers (one of them M. Leon Delaborde, the other an Englishman), both instructed by the magician of whom I am speaking, are stated to have succeeded in performing similar feats. But is it not almost certain, after what I have said, that those feats were accomplished by means of the suggestions of the interpreter or interpreters? Perhaps the same person who interpreted in the other cases which excited so much surprise did so in those also.

" I have stated all that I can for and against the magician, and leave it for others to decide upon the case. For myself, I am satisfied that his successes are to be attributed chiefly to the interpreter, but partly also to leading questions, and partly to mere guessing. Let us consider these three means as employed in one of the most remarkable cases. A number of individuals being called for, most of them (perhaps all), are correctly described. With the personal appearance of many of these individuals the interpreter is acquainted, and he is therefore able to suggest to the boy what he should say. When he has had no previous knowledge of the peculiarities of the appearance of a person called for, it has often happened that he has acquired such knowledge during the performance. One of the company, for instance, saying that he will call for such a person, adding that he is remarkable in such and such respects. When the first means cannot be employed, much may be done by the second, that is by leading questions. When a person having but one leg, or one leg shorter than another, is called for, he is perhaps vaguely described, and the boy is in consequence asked if there be anything peculiar in his legs : this question suggests to him that there *is* some peculiarity in his legs, and he probably ventures to say that he can only see *one* leg, then if this be unsatisfactory, he may add the person has turned rouud, and that he sees him to be *lame*. The third means (guessing) without the others is not likely to be of much service ; but with them it may help to supply trifling deficiencies, and when the guessing is wrong respecting a *trifling* matter, his *error* is considered trifling; but when he is right, his description is often considered striking for its *minute* accuracy.

" The last performances of this magician in my presence were ridiculous for their complete want of success. A woman was described as a man, a tall person as short or middle-sized, the very old as of a middle age, and so on. Two boys were employed; one was very stupid and appeared much frightened, the other seemed accustomed to the performance."

A friend has just described to me the latest performance of the magician, and you can hardly conceive anything more unfortunate and absurd. He had been sent for to gratify the curiosity of a party of English travellers at the French Hotel, a frequent scene of his impositions, where he often finds a boy ready to be employed by him, familiar with his tricks, and an interpreter disposed to aid his deceptions. A donkey-boy was sent for; and after the usual preparations, Lord Auckland was named as the first person whose image was to be presented to the boy, in the mirror of ink. He was merely described as short and thin. O'Connell was next represented as short and thin, dressed in white, young, without a beard, wearing a white hat with a handkerchief tied round it (like a Frank endeavouring to preserve his head from the heat of an Egyptian summer sun), and having only one

hand. Several other persons were called for, relations of individuals present, with various success;
and much laughter was occasioned, which made
the magician accuse the boy of not telling what he
saw. Another boy was sent for; and he seemed
to have been employed previously: sometimes he
got on before the magician. After many ridiculous failures, the Prince of Wales was described
with white hair, yellow beard, black coat, and
white trousers. (Beards, I should tell you, are
worn here by many European travellers.) The
party agreed not to laugh; and the names of persons present were given as those of individuals
whose images were required to appear. Sometimes
the image described was right in being tall, but
wrong in being fat: right as to coat, but wrong
as to trousers: just as you would expect in cases
of guessing. Five dollars were put upon a chair
before the magician; but he had the presence of
mind to wait for more, which, I believe, he received. I assure you he reaps a fine harvest from
the pockets of travellers.

If you wish to know what the performances of
this man were in earlier times, in the most remarkable instances, read an account of them in No. 117
of the "Quarterly Review;" and especially a note
there, following the remarks of the reviewer. You
will see, from what is there stated, that the subject
was deemed worthy of serious consideration, and

that a discovery of the means employed by the magician, which were thought to be of a very ingenious kind, was regarded as an interesting desideratum. That these means were not merely leading questions, and the like, as a late writer has suggested, is evident when we reflect that the magician is not known to have been even generally successful on any single occasion since the death of the interpreter 'Osmán, and it is not likely that intelligent travellers (of whom many might be named) would have been at a loss for the explanation, if such means would have sufficed.

One further remark I must make on this subject. If we give to some persons that credit which they are believed to deserve, we must admit that excited imagination, in the child employed as an agent in the deception, has sometimes produced images in the mirror of ink ; but these images have been always such as the child *expected* to see. The successful performances have been supposed, by some, to have been effected by means of mesmerism ; and some have attributed them to diabolical agency. As the grandest discoveries in science are often the most simple, so what appears to us at first most unaccountable is often capable of the most simple solution.

LETTER XXIX.

April, 1844.

MY DEAR FRIEND,

WHEN I promised you a description of the Bath, I did not anticipate that I should enter upon the subject with pleasure. Whatever others may think of it, I confess that the operation of bathing in the Eastern manner is to me extremely agreeable; and I have found it singularly beneficial in removing that lassitude which is occasioned by the climate. It is true that it is followed by a sense of fatigue, but a delightful repose soon ensues; and the consequences, upon the whole, I find almost as enjoyable as the process itself.

The buildings containing the baths are all nearly on the same plan, and are much alike in appearance; the fronts being decorated fancifully, in red and white, and the interiors consisting of several apartments paved with marble. I will describe to you, in a few words, one of the best in Cairo, which I visited with three ladies of my acquaintance,—English, Abyssinian, and Syrian.

After we had passed through two passages, we

found ourselves in the first large apartment, or
chamber of repose, in which the bathers undress
previously to their entering the heated chambers,
and in which they dress after taking the bath, and
rest on a raised marble platform, or wide bench,
on which are spread mats and carpets. In the
centre is a fountain of cold water, over which is a
dome. For a detailed account of the public baths
of Cairo I refer you to my brother's description;
and shall only relate to you the scenes through
which I passed on the occasion to which I have
referred.

In the first apartment, each of us enveloped herself in a very long and broad piece of drapery,
—which, but for its size, I might call a scarf,—and
proceeded through a small chamber, which was
moderately heated, to the principal inner apartment,
where the heat was intense. The plan of this apartment is that of a cross, having four recesses; each
of which, as well as the central portion, is covered
with a dome. The pavements are of white and
black marble, and small pieces of fine red tile, very
fancifully and prettily disposed. In the middle is
a jet of hot water, rising from the centre of a high
seat of marble, upon which many persons might
sit together. The pavement of each of the recesses
is a few inches higher than that of the central
portion of the apartment; and in one of them is a
trough, into which hot water was constantly pour-

ing from a pipe in the dome above. The whole apartment was full of steam.

On entering this chamber a scene presented itself which beggars description. My companions had prepared me for seeing many persons undressed; but imagine my astonishment on finding at least thirty women of all ages, and many young girls and children, perfectly unclothed. You will scarcely think it possible that no one but ourselves had a vestige of clothing. Persons of all colours, from the black and glossy shade of the negro to the fairest possible hue of complexion, were formed in groups, conversing as though full dressed, with perfect *nonchalance*, while others were strolling about, or sitting round the fountain. I cannot describe the bath as altogether a beautiful scene; in truth, in some respects it is disgusting; and I regret that I can never reach a private room in any bath without passing through the large public apartment.

. I will turn to the more agreeable subject—the operation of the bath, which is quite luxurious. The sensation experienced on first entering the hottest chamber is almost overpowering—the heat is extremely oppressive; and at first I believed that I could not long support such a temperature; but after the first minute, I was relieved by a gentle, and afterwards by a profuse perspiration, and no longer felt in any degree oppressed. It is always necessary for each lady to send her own bathing-linen, a pair of high clogs, a large copper vessel for hot water, two copper bowls, and towels.

The first operation is a gentle kneading the flesh, or champooing. Next the attendant cracks the joints of those who desire to submit to this process. I confess I did not suffer such an infliction. Some of the native women after this are rubbed with a rasp, or rather with two rasps of different kinds, a coarse one for the feet, and a fine one for the body; but neither of these rasps do I approve. A small coarse woollen bag, into which the operator's hand is inserted, is in my opinion preferable. Next the head and face are covered with a thick lather, which is produced by rubbing soap on a handful of fibres of the palm-tree, which are called leef, and which form a very agreeable and delicate-looking rubber. It is truly ridiculous to see another under this operation. When her head and face have been well lathered, and the soap has been thoroughly washed off by abundance of hot water, a novice would suppose that at least *they* were sufficiently purified; but this is not the case: two or three of such latherings, and as many washings, are necessary before the attendant thinks her duty to the head and face accomplished. Then follows the more agreeable part of the affair,—the general lathering and rubbing, which is performed by the attendant so gently, and in so pleasant a manner, that it is quite a luxury; and I am persuaded that the Eastern manner of bathing is highly salubrious, from its powerful effect upon the skin.

When the operation was completed, I was enveloped in a dry piece of drapery, similar to the bathing-dress, and conducted to the reposing-room, where I was rubbed and dressed, and left to take rest and refreshment, and to reflect upon the strange scene which I had witnessed. I wish I could say that there are no drawbacks to the enjoyment of the luxury I have described; but the eyes and ears of an Englishwoman must be closed in the public bath in Egypt before she can fairly enjoy the satisfaction it affords; for besides the very foreign scenes which cannot fail to shock her feelings of propriety, the cries of the children are deafening and incessant. The perfection of Eastern bathing is therefore rather to be enjoyed in a private bath, with the attendance of a practised velláneh.

LETTER XXX.

April, 1844.

MY DEAR FRIEND,

I REMEMBER writing, in my simplicity, that I believed Mohammad 'Alee Páshá to have but two wives; but having been introduced to another of his wives, the mother of Haleem Bey, in his hareem in the citadel, I conjecture that there is yet another, making the full Muslim allowance, namely, four wives.

The ride to the citadel is not an agreeable one, and at this time the ascent is attended with some danger, as the Páshá has directed the repair of the road leading from the Báb el Wezeer; in consequence of which heaps of stones and rubbish almost obstruct the way. I had chosen this route because it is unpaved, and my experience had made me dread the slippery paved entrance by the Great Gate, mounted, as I was, on a "high ass." Although expecting a tumble in riding over the rubbish, I could not help remarking the enormous size of some stones which had been thrown down from an old wall, so much resembling stones which scattered around the pyramids, that I do not d.r, they are some of those which were transported by Karakoosh when he was employed in building the citadel.

The Kasr appropriated to the hareem of the Páshá in the citadel is a noble mansion, the finest domestic structure I have seen in Egypt. The interior is on the usual Turkish plan. On the ground floor is a spacious saloon, paved with marble of a blueish white, nearly surrounded by suites of apartments which open into it; and on the first floor are rooms on the same plan. Accompanied by my friend Mrs. Sieder, I passed from the principal entrance to a large square court, and having crossed this, we found ourselves in the lower of the two saloons. We then ascended by an ample marble staircase to the saloon on the first floor. Here a most magnificent prospect burst upon our view: three windows which are opposite the head of the stairs, command the whole of Cairo, and the plain beyond; and every object of interest to the north and west of Cairo within the reach of our sight lay in picturesque variety before our admiring gaze; the green carpet of the Delta, and the plain of Goshen, terminating the view towards the north. I would willingly have lingered here, but our attendants were impatient to conduct us into the presence of the chief lady.

We found her sitting in a room which was carpeted and surrounded by a divan, attended by three

ladies. She received us with much respect and
cordiality, and as I had been informed that she had
the reputation of being an exceedingly haughty
person, I was agreeably surprised by finding in
her conversation and deportment the utmost affability and politeness. She conversed with me
freely of my children, told me that her son was
under twenty years of age, and introduced to my
notice two nice little girls, children of the hareem,
one of whom presented me with a *bouquet*. The
subject of the number, health, and age of each
lady's children is always the darling theme of conversation in the hareems, and truly to a mother
ever agreeable. One lady asked me with perfect
gravity, whether one of my boys, being thirteen
years of age, was married. I conclude she meant
betrothed, for the same word is used to express
marriage and betrothal. I explained to her that,
in England, a boy must become a man before he
thinks of marriage, or even betrothal; and that if
he entered into the marriage state at twenty years
of age, and a girl at fifteen, they would be considered too young. The lady whom I addressed,
and her companion, listened with much attention,
and one of them earnestly maintained that the English were quite right in objecting to such young
marriages as take place constantly in the East.

With respect to the beauties in this hareem, I
can only say that one was very remarkable; and

among the ornaments that I saw there, there was nothing deserving of particular notice excepting the pearl necklaces of the chief lady and two others: these were composed of the largest pearls that I have ever seen, but nearly tight round the throat.

On quitting this hareem, I was conducted by the ladies with the ceremony I have not described, which was that of holding the háberah on each side, while I crossed the saloons, and until I reached the hareem curtain. These attendant ladies, in imitation of their superiors, vied with each other in paying us every polite attention, and each and all in the hareem of the citadel were pictures of cheerfulness and good humour.

I was informed that no Franks had ever before been admitted into this hareem, and I believe it to be the case; though a portion of the same building, entered from the other side, and in which the Páshá has some rooms fitted up in the European manner, has been frequently seen by travellers. Some European ladies, a short time since, offered twenty dollars to procure admission, and were refused. I did not offer a bribe; for I never have condescended to obtain access to a hareem through the servants, and have either been introduced by my kind friend Mrs. Sieder, or paid my visit without any explanation to the slaves, and have never met with the slightest opposition. On quitting, it is necessary

to give a present to the chief eunuch, or to the
door-keeper.

After paying this visit, I called on my old
friends, the hareem of Habeeb Efendee; and I
confess I approached their house with some apprehension that, instead of their usual hearty welcome,
I might meet with a cold reception, during the
present state of things.   England and France
having lately required of the Sultán a concession
which every Christian must ardently desire, but
which it is almost impossible for him, as a Muslim
sovereign, to grant, and the result being not yet
known, it was particularly agreeable to our feelings,
in visiting his near relations, to find the whole
family prepared to welcome us with even more
than their usual affection.   The ladies in that
hareem being particularly well informed, the conversation during our visit takes always a lively,
and often a political turn ; and as soon as we were
seated yesterday, the passing events were discussed,
and the question of liberty of conscience on religious subjects soon introduced.   But here I must
digress, to remark to you one circumstance which
much pleased me.   While I was in conversation
with a lady who was sitting next to me, we both
heard the whole company, consisting of the
daughters and several visitors, suddenly rise, and,
following their example immediately, I observed

that the chief lady was entering the room. Very delightful is this outward respect for parents, which is not here, as in England, confined to a few of the families of the great; and when accompanied with that devotion of heart so evident in the conduct of the daughters of Habeeb Efendee. Their veneration for their amiable mother is complete; while they are permitted by her, in their conversation and manners, to indulge in the sweetest familiarity of affection.

This good lady saluted us in her usual charming manner, and took her seat, placing me, as she always has done, on her right hand; after which all resumed their places, and she listened with extreme interest to our conversation, which was translated to her into Turkish by her daughters. In common with all the Turkish ladies I have seen in this country, the wife of Habeeb Efendee speaks sufficient Arabic for the usual purposes of conversation; but when any particularly interesting topic is discussed, they all like it explained in their own language.

The eldest daughter requested to be informed particularly of the nature of the demand lately made by England and France on the Sultán; and when it was explained that he was required to protect from martyrdom such persons who, having been originally Christian, had become Muslims, and subsequently returned to their first profession, she replied, with an earnestness of manner which interested my friend and me extremely, " It is but the fulfilment of prophecy!   When I was a little child, I was taught that, in this year, great things would commence, which would require three years for their completion."

Surely she drew a beautiful conclusion, and under circumstances, too, of painful feelings to one strictly attached to the laws of her religion.   And here I must faithfully observe, that I have not met with this lady's equal in Eastern female society, in gentleness, sweetness, and good sense; and, withal, she has decidedly a cultivated mind.   The Hon. Mrs. Damer has very agreeably described this lady in her ' Tour,' and has particularly mentioned her affection for her mother.   I must not omit to tell you of the curiosity of the whole hareem on the subject of Mrs. Damer's book.   They had been informed that she had described them, and questioned us closely on the subject.   We had much pleasure in assuring them that the description in that lady's work consisted in honourable mention of her reception by the hareem, and of their agreeable manners, and perfect politeness and cordiality.   They inquired the exact period of her visit, that they might perfectly recall her to their recollection.   Secluded as they are, they remember the visits of Europeans.

as eras in their lives; and I am persuaded that they feel the pleasure they so agreeably express when we pay them a visit.

Mrs. Sieder has shown them the portrait of the present Sultán in Mrs. Damer's book; and the eldest daughter has made a copy of it in colours, very creditable to a Turkish lady. It will doubtless excite great interest in every visiter of the family; and, unless protected by a glass, it will perhaps, in the course of a few weeks, be kissed entirely away, like a miniature portrait of a Turkish grandee of which I was lately told.

NOTE BY THE EDITOR.

THIS Series of Letters somewhat abruptly terminates. The last letter, dated April, 1844, with several others, arrived from Cairo in May, and were delivered for publication. Since then, through some accidental circumstances, the communication has been interrupted. It is thought better to complete the volume with some illustrative matter, by way of Appendix, than to run the risk of any further delay.

August 23, 1844.

APPENDIX A.

[From Mr. Lane's ' Modern Egyptians.']

MAGIC.

A few days after my first arrival in this country, my curiosity was excited on the subject of magic by a circumstance related to me by Mr. Salt, our consul-general. Having had reason to believe that one of his servants was a thief, from the fact of several articles of property having been stolen from his house, he sent for a celebrated Maghrab'ee magician, with the view of intimidating them, and causing the guilty one (if any of them were guilty) to confess his crime. The magician came; and said that he would cause the exact image of the person who had committed the thefts to appear to any youth not arrived at the age of puberty; and desired the master of the house to call in any boy whom he might choose. As several boys were then employed in a garden adjacent to the house, one of them was called for this purpose. In the palm of this boy's right hand the magician drew, with a pen, a certain diagram, in the centre of which he poured a little ink. Into this ink he desired the boy steadfastly to look. He then burned some incense and several bits of paper inscribed with charms; and, at the same time, called for various objects to appear in the ink. The boy declared that he saw all these objects, and, last of all, the image of the guilty person: he described

I 3

his stature, countenance, and dress; said that he knew him;
and directly ran down into the garden, and apprehended one
of the labourers, who, when brought before the master, immediately confessed that he was the thief.

The above relation made me desirous of witnessing a similar performance during my first visit to this country; but
not being acquainted with the name of the magician here
alluded to, or his place of abode, I was unable to obtain any
tidings of him.   I learned, however, soon after my return to
England, that he had become known to later travellers in
Egypt; was residing in Cairo; and that he was called the
sheykh 'Abd-El-Kádir El-Maghrab'ee. A few weeks after
my second arrival in Egypt, my neighbour 'Osmán, interpreter of the British consulate, brought him to me; and
I fixed a day for his visiting me, to give me a proof of the
skill for which he is so much famed. He came at the time
appointed, about two hours before noon; but seemed uneasy;
frequently looked up at the sky, through the window; and
remarked that the weather was unpropitious; it was dull
and cloudy, and the wind was boisterous. The experiment
was performed with three boys; one after another. With
the first, it was partly successful; but with the others, it
completely failed. The magician said that he could do
nothing more that day; and that he would come in the evening of a subsequent day. He kept his appointment; and
admitted that the time was favourable. While waiting
for my neighbour, before mentioned, to come and witness
the performances, we took pipes and coffee; and the magician chatted with me on indifferent subjects. He is a fine,
tall, and stout man, of a rather fair complexion, with a dark
brown beard; is shabbily dressed; and generally wears a
large green turban, being a descendant of the prophet. In
his conversation, he is affable and unaffected. He professed

to me that his wonders were effected by the agency of *good* spirits; but to others, he has said the reverse—that his magic is Satanic.

. In preparing for the experiment of the magic mirror of ink, which, like some other performances of a similar nature, is here termed *darb el-mendel*, the magician first asked me for a reed-pen and ink, a piece of paper, and a pair of scissors; and, having cut off a narrow strip of paper, wrote upon it certain forms of invocation, together with another charm, by which he professes to accomplish the object of the experiment. He did not attempt to conceal these; and on my asking him to give me copies of them, he readily consented, and immediately wrote them for me; explaining to me, at the same time, that the object he had in view was accomplished through the influence of the two first words, " Tarshun " and " Taryooshun," which, he said, were the names of two genii, his " familiar spirits." I compared the copies with the originals; and found that they exactly agreed.

" Tarshun! Taryooshun! Come down!
Come down! Be present! Whither are gone
the prince and his troops? Where are El-Ahmar
the prince and his troops? Be present,
ye servants of these names!"

" And this is the removal. ' And we have removed from thee
thy veil; and thy sight to-day
is piercing.' Correct: correct."

Having written these, the magician cut off the paper containing the forms of invocation from that upon which the other charm was written; and cut the former into six strips. He then explained to me that the object of the latter charm (which contains part of the 21st verse of the Soorat Káf,

or 50th chapter of the Kur-án) was to open the boy's eyes
in a supernatural manner; to make his sight pierce into
what is to us the invisible world.

I had prepared, by the magician's direction, some frankincense and coriander-seed,* and a chafing-dish with some
live charcoal in it. These were now brought into the room,
together with the boy who was to be employed: he had been
called in, by my desire, from among some boys in the street,
returning from a manufactory; and was about eight or nine
years of age. In reply to my inquiry respecting the description of persons who could see in the magic mirror of ink, the
magician said that they were a boy not arrived at puberty, a
virgin, a black female slave, and a pregnant woman. The
chafing-dish was placed before him and the boy; and the
latter was placed on a seat. The magician now desired my
servant to put some frankincense and coriander-seed into the
chafing-dish; then, taking hold of the boy's right hand, he
drew, in the palm of it, a magic square, of which a copy is
here given. The figures which it contains are Arabic nume-
rals.† In the centre, he poured a little ink, and desired the
boy to look into it, and tell him if he could see his face
reflected in it; the boy replied that he saw his face clearly.

* He generally requires some benzoin to be added to these.
† The numbers in this magic square, in our own ordinary characters,
are as follows :—

4	9	2
3	5	7
8	1	6

It will seen that the horizontal, vertical, and diagonal rows give each,
the same sum, namely, 15.

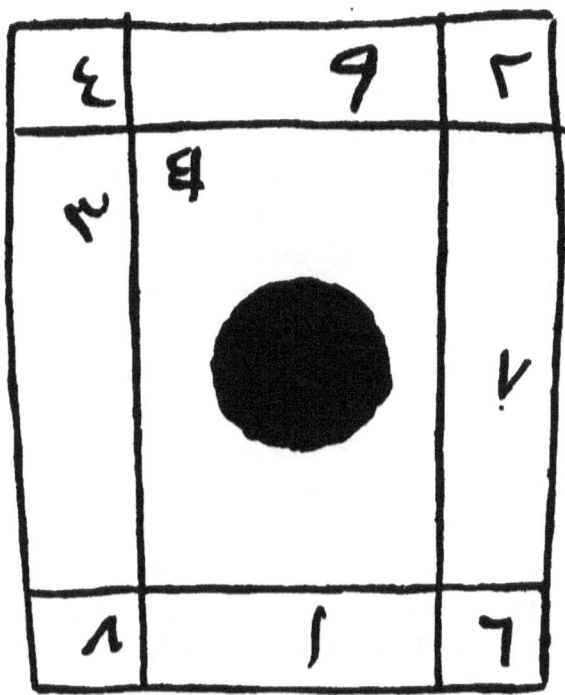

Magic Diagram and Mirror of Ink.

The magician, holding the boy's hand all the while,* told him to continue looking intently into the ink; and not to raise his head.

He then took one of the little strips of paper inscribed with the forms of invocation, and dropped it into the chafing-dish, upon the burning coals and perfumes, which had already filled the room with their smoke; and as he did this, he commenced an indistinct muttering of words, which he continued during the whole process, excepting when he had to ask the boy a question, or to tell him what he was to say. The piece of paper containing the words from the Kur-án, he placed inside the fore part of the boy's tákeeyeh, or skull-cap. He then asked him if he saw anything in the ink; and

* This reminds us of animal magnetism.

was answered " No:" but about a minute after, the boy, trembling, and seeming much frightened, said, " I see a man sweeping the ground." " When he has done sweeping," said the magician, " tell me." Presently the boy said, " He has done." The magician then again interrupted his muttering to ask the boy if he knew what a *beyrak* (or flag) was; and being answered " Yes," desired him to say, " Bring a flag." The boy did so; and soon said, " He has brought a flag." " What colour is it?" asked the magician: the boy replied " Red." He was told to call for another flag; which he did; and soon after he said that he saw another brought; and that it was black. In like manner, he was told to call for a third, fourth, fifth, sixth, and seventh; which he described as being successively brought before him; specifying their colours, as white, green, black, red, and blue. The magician then asked him (as he did, also, each time that a new flag was described as being brought), " How many flags have you now before you?" " Seven," answered the boy. While this was going on, the magician put the second and third of the small strips of paper upon which the forms of invocation were written, into the chafing-dish; and, fresh frankincense and coriander-seed having been repeatedly added, the fumes became painful to the eyes. When the boy had described the seven flags as appearing to him, he was desired to say, " Bring the Sultán's tent; and pitch it." This he did; and in about a minute after, he said, " Some men have brought the tent; a large green tent: they are pitching it;" and presently he added, " they have set it up." " Now," said the magician, " order the soldiers to come, and to pitch their camp around the tent of the Sultán." The boy did as he was desired; and immediately said, " I see a great many soldiers, with their tents: they have pitched their tents." He was then told to order that the soldiers should be drawn up in ranks; and, having done so, he presently said, that he saw them thus arranged. The magician had put the fourth of the little strips of paper into the chafing-dish; and soon after, he did the same with the fifth. He now said, " Tell some of the people to bring a bull." The boy gave the order required, and said, " I see a bull : it is red : four men are dragging it along; and three are beating it." He was told to desire them to kill it, and cut it up, and to put the meat in saucepans, and cook it. He did as he was directed; and described these operations as apparently performed before his eyes. " Tell the soldiers," said the magician, "to eat it." The boy did so; and said, " They are eating it. They have done; and are washing their hands." The magician then told him to call for the Sultán; and the boy, having done this, said, " I see the Sultán riding to his tent, on a bay horse; and he has on his head a high red cap: he has alighted at his tent, and sat down within it." " Desire them to bring coffee to the Sultán," said the magician, " and to form the court." These orders were given by the boy; and he said that he saw them performed. The magician had put the last of the six little strips of paper into the chafing-dish. In his mutterings I distinguished nothing but the words of the written invocation, frequently repeated, excepting on two or three occasions, when I heard him say, " If they demand information, inform them; and be ye veracious." But much that he repeated was inaudible, and as I did not ask him to teach me his art, I do not pretend to assert that I am fully acquainted with his invocations.

He now addressed himself to me; and asked me if I wished the boy to see any person who was absent or dead. I named Lord Nelson; of whom the boy had evidently never heard; for it was with much difficulty that he pronounced the name, after several trials. The magician desired the boy to say to the Sultán—" My master salutes thee, and desires thee to bring Lord Nelson: bring him before my eyes, that I may see him, speedily." The boy then said so; and almost immediately added, " A messenger is gone, and has returned, and brought a man, dressed in a black* suit of European clothes: the man has lost his left arm." He then paused for a moment or two; and, looking more intently, and more closely into the ink, said, " No, he has not lost his left arm; but it is placed to his breast." This correction made his description more striking than it had been without it: since Lord Nelson generally had his empty sleeve attached to the breast of his coat: but it was the *right* arm that he had lost. Without saying that I suspected the boy had made a mistake, I asked the magician whether the objects appeared in the ink as if actually before the eyes, or as if in a glass, which makes the right appear left. He answered, that they appeared as in a mirror. This rendered the boy's description faultless.†

The next person I called for was a native of Egypt, who has been for many years resident in England, where he has adopted our dress; and who had been long confined to his bed by illness before I embarked for this country: I thought that his name, one not very uncommon in Egypt, might

---

* Dark blue is called, by the modern Egyptians, *eswed*, which properly signifies *black*, and is therefore so translated here.

† Whenever I desired the boy to call for any person to appear, I paid particular attention both to the magician and to 'Osmán. The latter gave no direction either by word or sign; and indeed he was generally unacquainted with the personal appearance of the individual called for. I took care that he had no previous communication with the boys; and have seen the experiment fail when he *could* have given directions to them, or to the magician. In short, it would be difficult to conceive any precaution which I did not take. It is important to add, that the dialect of the magician was more intelligible to me than to the boy. When *I* understood him perfectly at once, he was sometimes obliged to vary his words to make the *boy* comprehend what he said.

make the boy describe him incorrectly; though another boy, on the former visit of the magician, had described this same person as wearing a European dress, like that in which I last saw him. In the present case the boy said, " Here is a man brought on a kind of bier, and wrapped up in a sheet." This description would suit, supposing the person in question to be still confined to his bed, or if he be dead.* The boy described his face as covered; and was told to order that it should be uncovered. This he did; and then said, " His face is pale; and he has mustaches, but no beard :" which is correct.

Several other persons were successively called for; but the boy's descriptions of them were imperfect; though not altogether incorrect. He represented each object as appearing less distinct than the preceding one; as if his sight were gradually becoming dim: he was a minute, or more, before he could give any account of the persons he professed to see towards the close of the performance; and the magician said it was useless to proceed with him. Another boy was then brought in; and the magic square, &c. made in his hand; but he could see nothing. The magician said he was too old.

Though completely puzzled, I was somewhat disappointed with his performances, for they fell short of what he had accomplished, in many instances, in presence of certain of my friends and countrymen. On one of these occasions, an Englishman present ridiculed the performance, and said that nothing would satisfy him but a correct description of the appearance of his own father, of whom, he was sure, no one of the company had any knowledge. The boy, accord-

---

* A few months after this was written, I had the pleasure of hearing that the person here alluded to was in better health. Whether he was confined to his bed at the time when this experiment was performed, I have not been able to ascertain.

ingly, having called by name for the person alluded to, described a man in a Frank dress, with his hand placed to his head, wearing spectacles, and with one foot on the ground, and the other raised behind him, as if he were stepping down from a seat. The description was exactly true in every respect: the peculiar position of the hand was occasioned by an almost constant head-ache: and that of the foot or leg, by a stiff knee, caused by a fall from a horse, in hunting. I am assured that, on this occasion, the boy accurately described each person and thing that was called for. On another occasion, Shakspere was described with the most minute correctness, both as to person and dress; and I might add several other cases in which the same magician has excited astonishment in the sober minds of Englishmen of my acquaintance. A short time since, after performing in the usual manner, by means of a boy, he prepared the magic mirror in the hand of a young English lady, who, on looking into it for a little while, said that she saw a broom sweeping the ground without anybody holding it, and was so much frightened that she would look no longer.

I have stated these facts partly from my own experience, and partly as they came to my knowledge on the authority of respectable persons. The reader may be tempted to think that, in each instance, the boy saw images produced by some reflection in the ink; but this was evidently not the case; or that he was a confederate, or guided by leading questions. That there was no collusion, I satisfactorily ascertained, by selecting the boy who performed the part above described in my presence from a number of others passing by in the street, and by his rejecting a present which I afterwards offered him with the view of inducing him to confess that he did not really see what he had professed to have seen. I tried the veracity of another boy on a subsequent occasion in the same manner; and the result was the same. The experiment often entirely fails; but when the boy employed is right in one case, he generally is so in all: when he gives, at first, an account altogether wrong, the magician usually dismisses him at once, saying that he is too old. The perfumes, or excited imagination, or fear, may be supposed to affect the vision of the boy who describes objects as appearing to him in the ink; but, if so, why does he see exactly what is required, and objects of which he can have had no previous particular notion? Neither I nor others have been able to discover any clue by which to penetrate the mystery; and if the reader be alike unable to give the solution, I hope that he will not allow the above account to induce in his mind any degree of scepticism with respect to other portions of this work.*

* It has been suggested (in the 'Quarterly Review,' No. 117) that the performances were effected by means of pictures and a concave mirror; and that the images of the former were reflected from the surface of the mirror, and received on a cloud of smoke under the eyes of the boy. This, however, I cannot admit; because such means could not have been employed without my perceiving them; nor would the images be *reversed* (unless the pictures were so) by being reflected from the surface of a mirror, and received upon a *second surface;* for the boy was looking *down* upon the palm of his hand, so that an image could not be formed upon the smoke (which was copious, but not dense) between his eye and the supposed mirror.

APPENDIX B.

[From Mr. Lane's ' Modern Egyptians.']

FEMALE ORNAMENTS.

THE ornaments of the women of Egypt are so various, that
a description of them all would far exceed the limits which
the nature of this work allows, and would require a great
number of engravings, or be useless. I shall, however, describe all the principal kinds; and these will convey some
idea of the rest. If the subject be not interesting to general
readers, it may at least be of some use to artists, who are
often left almost entirely to their own imagination in representing Arabian costumes and ornaments. I first describe
those which are worn by *ladies*, and females of the *middle
orders*.

The head-dress has already been mentioned, as composed
of a "tarboosh" and "faroodeeyeh" (or kerchief), which
latter, when wound round the former, is called "rabtah."
The front part of the rabtah is often ornamented with
spangles of gilt or plain silver, disposed in fanciful patterns;
and in this case, the rabtah itself is generally of black or
rose-coloured muslin or crape, and always plain. The more
common kinds of rabtah have been described.

The "mizágee" is an ornament very generally worn. It
is composed of a strip of muslin, most commonly black or
rose-coloured, folded together several times, so as to form a

narrow band, about the breadth of a finger, or less. Its length is about five feet. The central part, for the space of about twelve or thirteen inches, is ornamented with spangles, which are placed close together, or in the form of diamonds, &c., or of bosses; and at each end, for about the same length, are a few other spangles, with an edging, and small tassels, of various coloured silks. Sometimes there is also a similar edging, with spangles suspended to it, along the lower edge of the ornamented part in the middle. The mizágee is bound round the head; the ornamented central part being over the forehead, generally above the edge of the rabtah: it is tied behind, at the upper part of the rabtah; and the ornamented ends, drawn forward, hang over the bosom.

The "kurs" is a round, convex ornament, commonly about five inches in diameter; which is very generally worn by ladies. It is sowed upon the crown of the tarboosh. There are two kinds. The first that I shall describe (the

Diamond Kurs.

only kind that is worn by ladies, or by the wives of tradesmen of moderate property) is the "kurs almás," or diamond
kurs. This is composed of diamonds; set generally in gold;
and is of open work, representing roses, leaves, &c. The
diamonds are commonly of a very poor and shallow kind;
and the gold of this and all other diamond ornaments worn
in Egypt is much alloyed with copper. The value of a moderately handsome diamond kurs is about a hundred and
twenty-five or a hundred and fifty pounds sterling. It is
very seldom made of silver; and I think that those of gold,
when attached to the deep-red tarboosh, have a richer effect,
though not in accordance with our general taste. The
wives even of petty tradesmen sometimes wear the diamond
kurs: they are extremely fond of diamonds, and generally
endeavour to get some, however bad. The kurs, being of
considerable weight, is at first painful to wear; and women
who are in the habit of wearing it complain of headache
when they take it off; hence they retain it day and night;
but some have an inferior one for the bed. Some ladies
have one for ordinary wearing; another for particular occa-

Gold Kurs.

sions, a little larger and handsomer; and a third merely to wear in bed.—The other kind of kurs, "kurs dahab" (or, of gold), is a convex plate of very thin embossed gold, usually of the form represented above; and almost always with a false emerald (a piece of green glass), not cut with facets, set in the centre. Neither the emerald nor the ruby is here cut with facets: if so cut, they would generally be considered false. The simple gold kurs is lined with a thick coat of wax, which is covered with a piece of paper. It is worn by many women who cannot afford to purchase diamonds; and even by some servants.

The kussah is an ornament generally from seven to eight inches in length, composed of diamonds set in gold, and sometimes with emeralds, rubies, and pearls; having drops of diamonds or emeralds, &c., suspended to it. It is worn on the front of the rabtah, attached by little hooks at the back. I have seen several kussahs of diamonds, &c., set in silver instead of gold. The kussah is generally placed on the head of a bride, outside her shawl covering; as also is the kurs; and these ornaments are likewise employed to decorate the bier of a female. The former, like the latter, is worn by females of the higher and middle classes.

"'Enebeh" is another name for the same kind of ornament, worn in the same manner. If of full size, it is fourteen or fifteen inches in length; and rather more than half encircles the head-dress.

The "shawáteh" (in the singular, "sháteh") are two ornaments, each consisting of three or more strings of pearls, about the length of the kussah, with a pierced emerald uniting them in the centre, like the usual pearl necklace hereafter described; or they are composed of pearls arranged in the manner of a narrow lace, and often with the addition of a few small emeralds. They are attached to the rabtah in the

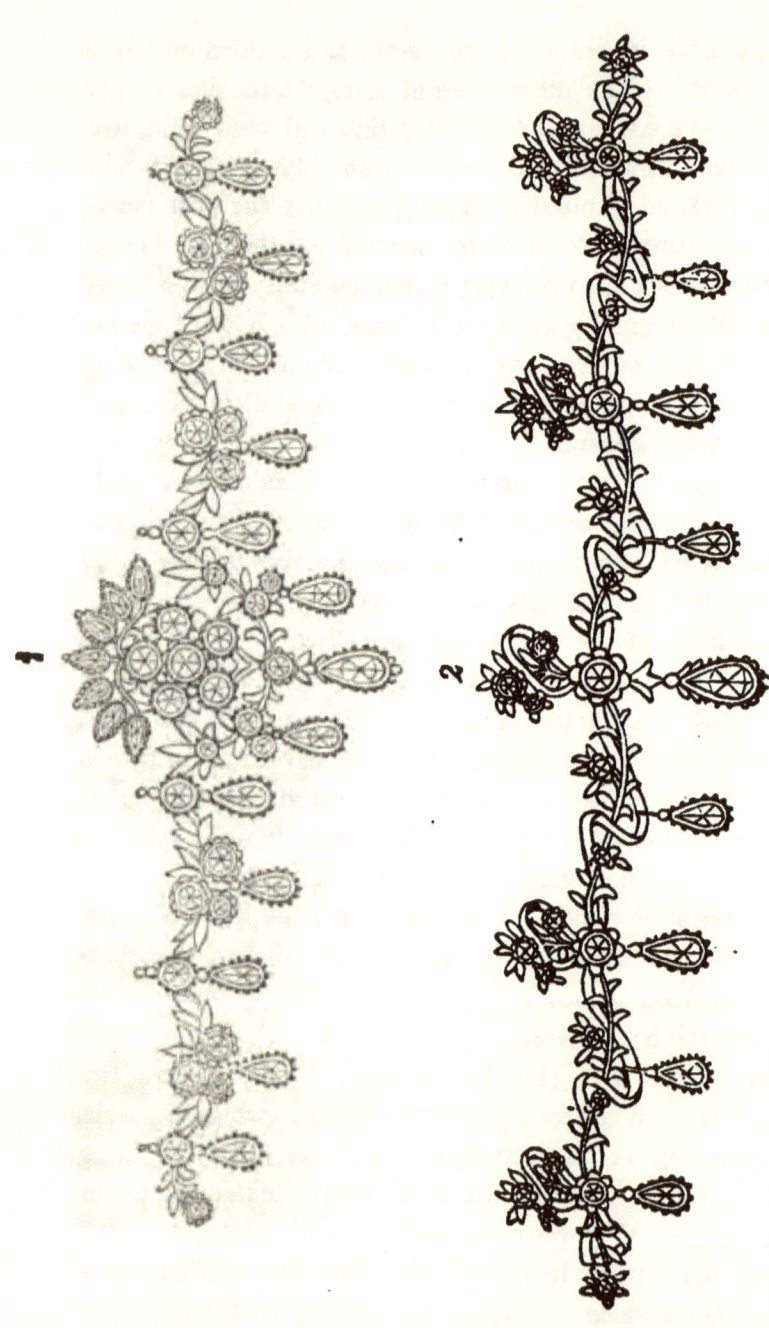

1. Kusah; 2. 'Enebeh; the former half, and the latter one-third, of the real size.

form of two festoons, one on each side of the head, from the extremity of the kussah to the back part of the head-dress, or, sometimes, to the ear-ring.

Instead of the kussah and shawáteh, and sometimes in addition to them, are worn some other ornaments which I proceed to describe.

The "reesheh" (literally, "feather") is a sprig of diamonds set in gold or silver. It is worn on the front or side of the head-dress.

The "hilál" is a crescent of diamonds set in gold or silver, and worn like the reesheh. In form it resembles the phasis of the moon when between two and three nights old; its width being small, and its outward edge not more than half a circle.

The "kamarah" (or moon) is an ornament formed of a thin plate of gold, embossed with fanciful work, and sometimes with Arabic words, and having about seven little flat pieces of gold, called "bark," attached to the lower part; or it is composed of gold with diamonds, rubies, &c. Two specimens of the former kind are represented in the following page. One of these consists of three kamarahs connected together, to be worn on the front of the head-dress: the central contains the words "Yá Káfee Yá Sháfee" (O Sufficient! O Restorer to health!): that on the left, "Yá Háfiz" (O Preserver!): that on the right, "Yá Emeen" (O Trustworthy!): these, therefore, are charms as well as ornaments.

The "sákiyeh" (or water-wheel), so called from its form, is a circular flat ornament of gold filigree-work, with small pearls, and with a diamond or other precious stone in the centre, and bark and emeralds suspended from the lower part. It is worn in the same manner as the kamarah, or with the latter ornament.

The "'ood es-saleeb" (or wood of the cross) is a kind of

K

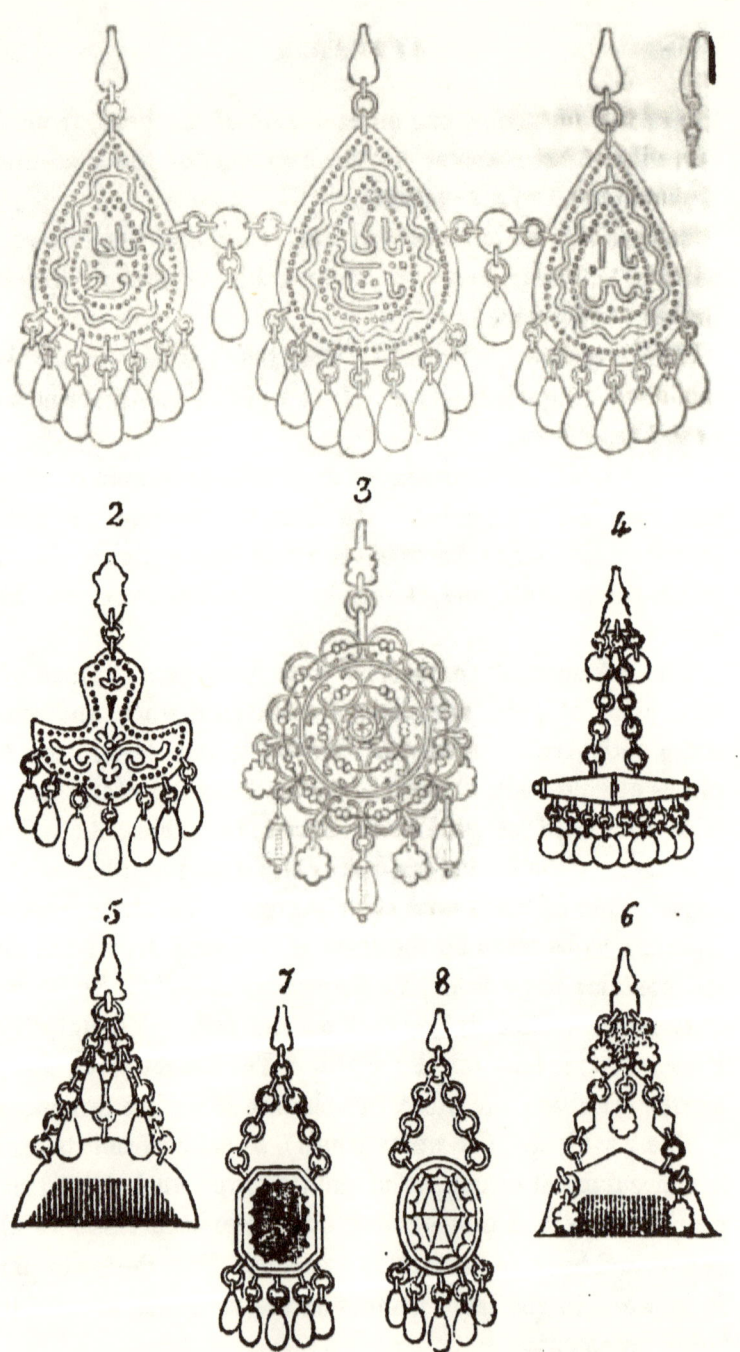

1 and 2. Kamarahs. 3. Sákiyeh. 4. 'Ood es-Saleeb. 5 and 6. Mishts.
7. 'Akeek. 8. Belloor. Each half the real size.

ornament undoubtedly borrowed from the Christians; and it is surprising that Mohammadan women should wear it, and give it this appellation. It is a little round and slender piece of wood, rather smaller towards the extremities than in the middle, enclosed in a case of gold, of the same form, composed of two pieces which unite in the middle, having two chains and a hook by which to suspend it, and a row of bark along the bottom. It is worn in the place of, or with, the two ornaments just before described.

The "misht" (or comb) is a little comb of gold, worn in the same manner as the three kinds of ornament described next before this, and generally with one or more of those ornaments. It is suspended by small chains and a hook, having four or five bark attached.

There is also an ornament somewhat similar to those just mentioned, composed of a cornelian, or a piece of crystal or of colourless glass, set in gold, suspended by two chains and a hook, and having bark attached to the bottom. The former kind is called "'akeek" (which signifies "cornelian"), and the latter, "belloor" ("crystal").

Several ornaments in the shapes of flowers, butterflies, &c. are also worn upon the head-dress; but seldom alone.

Of ear-rings ("halak") there is a great variety. Some of the more usual kinds are here represented. The first is of a diamond set in silver. It consists of a drop suspended within a wreath hanging from a sprig. The back of the silver is gilt, to prevent its being tarnished by perspiration. The specimen here given is that for the right ear: its fellow is similar; but with the sprig reversed. This pair of ear-rings is suited for a lady of wealth.—So also is the second, which resembles the former, excepting that it has a large pearl in the place of the diamond drop and wreath, and that the diamonds of the sprig are set in gold. No. 3 is a side view of the same.—The next consists of gold, and an emerald pierced through the middle, with a small diamond above the emerald. Emeralds are generally pierced in Egypt, and

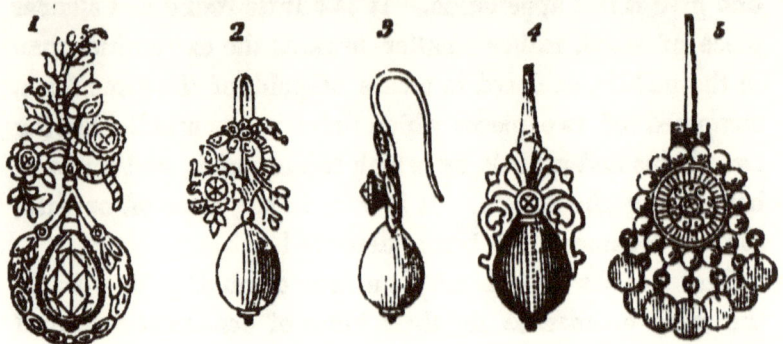

Ear-rings—each half the real size.

spoiled by this process as much as by not being cut with facets. —The last is of gold, with a small ruby in the centre. The ruby is set in fine filigree-work, which is surrounded by fifteen balls of gold. To the seven lower balls are suspended as many circular bark.

The necklace ("'ekd") is another description of ornament of which the Egyptians have a great variety; but almost all of them are similar in the following particulars. 1st. The beads, &c., of which they are composed are, altogether, not more than ten inches in length; so that they would not entirely encircle the neck if tied quite tight, which is never done; the string extends about six or seven inches beyond ʳch extremity of the series of beads; and when the neck- ᵍ is tied in the usual manner, there is generally a space inches or more between these extremities; but ᶠ hair conceal these parts of the string. 2ndly. ʳally, in the centre, one bead or other orna- ᵐᵉˢ there are three, or five, or seven) ᶜ material, or colour from the others.— ʳorn by ladies are of diamonds or

1 and 2. Kamarahs. 3. Sákiyeh.
7. 'Akeek. 8. Belloor.

pearls. There is also a long kind of necklace, reaching to
the girdle, and composed of diamonds or other precious
stones, which is called "kiládeh." Some women form a long
necklace of this kind with Venetian sequins, or Turkish or
Egyptian gold coins.

The finger-rings ("khátims") differ so little from those
common among ourselves, excepting in the clumsiness of
their workmanship, and the badness of the jewels, that I
need not describe them. A finger-ring without a stone is
called "debleh," or "dibleh."

Bracelets ("asáwir") are of diamonds or other precious
stones set in gold, or of pearls, or of gold alone. The more
common kinds are represented in an engraving here inserted.—No. 1 is a side view of a diamond bracelet, with a
front view of a portion of the same.—No. 2 is the most
fashionable kind of gold bracelet, which is formed of a
simple twist.—No. 3 is a very common, but less fashionable
kind of bracelet of twisted gold. No. 4 is also of gold.—
These bracelets of gold are pulled open a little to be put on
the wrist. They are generally made of fine Venetian gold,
which is very flexible.

The ornaments of the *hair* I shall next describe.—It has
been mentioned, that all the hair of the head, excepting a
little over the forehead and temples, is arranged in plaits,
or braids, which hang down the back. These plaits are
generally from eleven to twenty-five in number ; but always
of an uneven number: eleven is considered a scanty number: thirteen and fifteen are more common. Three times
the number of black silk strings (three to each plait of hair,
and each united at the top), from sixteen to eighteen inches
in length, are braided with the hair for about a quarter of
their length ; or they are attached to a lace or band of black
silk which is bound round the head, and in this case hang

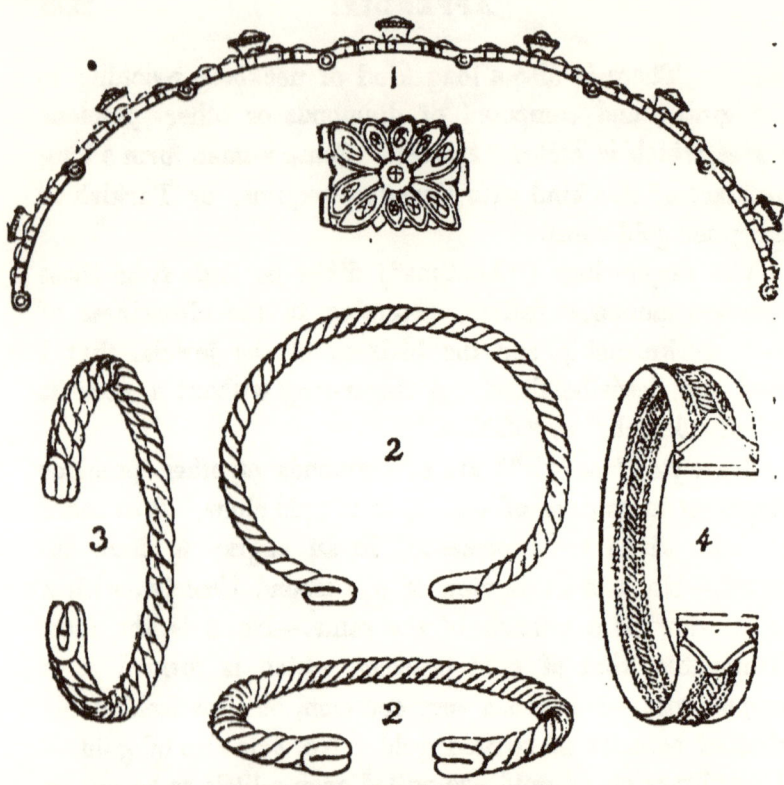

Bracelets—each half the real size.

entirely separate from the plaits of hair, which they almost
conceal. These strings are called "keytáns;" and together
with certain ornaments of gold, &c., the more common of
which are here represented, compose what is termed the

1, 2, 3, 4. Bark.   5. Másoorah.   6. Habbeh.   7. Shiftish'eh.
Each half the real size.

"safa." Along each string, excepting from the upper
extremity to about a quarter or (at most) a third of its
length, are generally attached nine or more of the little flat

ornaments of gold called "bark." These are commonly all of the same form, and about an inch, or a little more, apart; but those of each string are purposely placed so as not exactly to correspond with those of the others. The most usual forms of bark are Nos. 1 and 2 of the specimens given above. At the end of each string is a small gold tube, called "másoorah," about three-eighths of an inch long, or a kind of gold bead in the form of a cube with a portion cut off from each angle, called "habbeh." Beneath the másoorah or habbeh is a little ring, to which is most commonly suspended a Turkish gold coin called "Ruba Fenduklee," equivalent to nearly 1s. 8d. of our money, and a little more than half an inch in diameter. Such is the most general description of safa; but there are more genteel kinds, in which the habbeh is usually preferred to the másoorah, and instead of the Ruba Fenduklee is a flat ornament of gold, called, from its form, "kummetrë," or "pear." There are also other and more approved substitutes for the gold coin; the most usual of which is called "shiftish'eh," composed of open gold work, with a pearl in the centre. Some ladies substitute a little tassel of pearls for the gold coin; or suspend alternately pearls and emeralds to the bottom of the triple strings; and attach a pearl with each of the bark. The safa thus composed with pearls is called "safa loolee." Coral beads are also sometimes attached in the same manner as the pearls.—From what has been said above, it appears that a moderate safa of thirteen plaits will consist of 39 strings, 351 bark, 39 másoorahs or habbehs, and 39 gold coins or other ornaments; and that a safa of twenty-five plaits, with twelve bark to each string, will contain no fewer than 900 bark, and 75 of each of the other appendages. The safa appears to me the prettiest, as well as the most singular, of all the ornaments worn by the ladies of Egypt.

The glittering of the bark, &c., and their chinking together as the wearer walks, have a peculiarly lively effect.

Anklets ("khulkhál"), of solid gold or silver, and of the form here sketched, are worn by some ladies; but are more

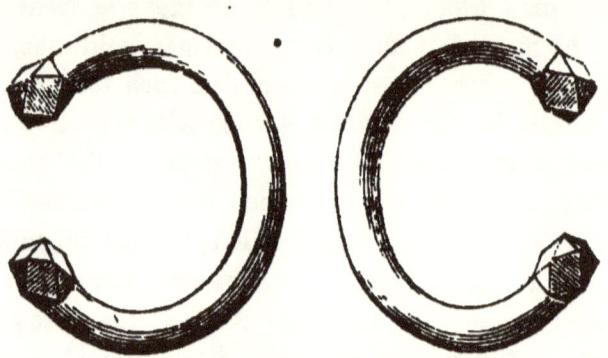

Anklets—one-fourth of the real size.

uncommon than they formerly were. They are of course very heavy, and, knocking together as the wearer walks, make a ringing noise; hence it is said in a song, "The ringing of thine anklets has deprived me of my reason." Isaiah alludes to this,* or perhaps to the sound produced by another kind of anklet which will be mentioned hereafter.

The only description of ladies' ornaments that I have yet to describe is the "hegáb," or amulet. This is a writing covered with wax cloth, to preserve it from accidental pollution, or injury by moisture, and enclosed in a case of thin embossed gold or silver, which is attached to a silk string, or a chain, and generally hung on the right side, above the girdle; the string or chain being passed over the left shoulder. Sometimes these cases bear Arabic inscriptions; such as "Má-sháa-lláh" ("What God willeth [cometh to pass]") and "Yá kadi-l-hágát" ("O decreer of the things that are needful!"). I insert an engraving of three hegábs of gold,

* Chap. iii. ver. 16.

attached to a string, to be worn together. The central one is a thin, flat case, containing a folded paper: it is about a

Hegábs—one fourth of the real size.

third of an inch thick: the others are cylindrical cases, with hemispherical ends, and contain scrolls: each has a row of bark along the bottom. Hegábs such as these, or of a triangular form, are worn by many children, as well as women; and those of the latter form are often attached to a child's head-dress.

The ornaments worn by females of the *lower orders* must now be described.

It is necessary, perhaps, to remind the reader, that the head-dress of these women, with the exception of some of the poor in the villages, generally consists of an 'asbeh'; and that some wear, instead of this, the tarboosh and faroodeeyeh. Sometimes a string of Venetian sequins (which is called " sheddeh benád'kah") is worn along the front of the 'asbeh or rabtah. The tarboosh is also sometimes decorated with the gold kurs and the faroodeeyeh, with some other ornaments before described, as the gold kamarahs, sakiyeh, misht, &c.

The "halak," or ear-rings, are of a great variety of forms

K 3

Some are of gold and precious stones; but the more common of brass; and many of the latter have coloured beads attached to them. A few are of silver.

The "khizám," or nose-ring, commonly called "khuzám," is worn by a few of the women of the lower orders in Cairo, and by many of those in the country towns and villages both of Upper and Lower Egypt. It is most commonly made of brass; is from an inch to an inch and a half in diameter; and has usually three or more coloured glass beads, generally red and blue, attached to it. It is almost always

Nose-rings—half the real size.

passed through the right ala of the nose; and hangs partly before the mouth; so that the wearer is obliged to hold it up with one hand when she puts anything into her mouth. It is sometimes of gold. This ornament is as ancient as the time of the patriarch Abraham;* and is mentioned by Isaiah† and by Ezekiel.‡ To those who are unaccustomed to the sight of it, the nose-ring is certainly the reverse of an ornament.   •

* See Genesis xxiv. 47, where in our common version, "ear-ring" is improperly put for " nose-ring."

† Chap. iii. ver. 21.

‡ Chap. xvi. ver. 12. Here, again, a mistake is made in our common version, but corrected in the margin.

The "'ekd," or necklace, is generally of a style similar to those which I have already described. I have before mentioned that the libbeh and sha'eer are worn by some women of the lower orders; but their necklaces are most commonly composed of coloured glass beads; sometimes, of a single string; and sometimes, of several strings, with one or more larger beads in the centre: or they are made in the form of net-work. The Egyptian women, being excessively fond of ornaments, often wear two or three necklaces of the value of a penny each, or less. Some necklaces are composed of large beads of transparent amber.

Another ornament worn by many of them on the neck is a ring, called "tók," of silver or brass or pewter. Little girls, also, sometimes wear this ornament. Some of the smaller tóks are made of iron.

Tok, or Neck-ring—one-fourth of the real size.

Finger-rings of silver or of brass are almost universally

worn. Brass rings, with pieces of coloured glass set in them, may be purchased in Cairo for scarcely more than a farthing each; and many women wear two, three, or more, of these.

The "asáwir," or bracelets, are of various kinds. Some are of silver; and some of brass or copper; and of the same form as those of gold before described. Those of brass are the more common. There are also bracelets composed of large amber beads, and others of bone; and there is a very common kind, called "ghuweyshát," of opaque, coloured glass, generally blue or green, but sometimes variegated with other colours. These, and the bone bracelets, are drawn over the hand.

Some of the women of the lower orders imitate their superiors in arranging their hair in several plaits, and plaiting, with each of these, the black silk strings which are worn by the ladies; but it is the general practice of the women of these classes to divide their hair into only two tresses behind, and to plait, with each of these tresses, three red silk strings, each of which has a tassel at the end, and reaches more than half way towards the ground; so that they are usually obliged to draw aside the tassel before they sit down. These appendages are called "'okoos."

"Khulkhál," or anklets of solid silver, already described, are worn by the wives of some of the richer peasants, and of the sheykhs of villages; and small khulkháls of iron are worn by many children. It was also a common custom among the Arabs, for girls or young women to wear a string of bells on their feet. I have seen many little girls in Cairo with small round bells attached to their anklets. Perhaps it is to the sound of ornaments of this kind, rather than that of the more common anklet, that Isaiah alludes in chapter iii. verse 16.

APPENDIX C.

[The description of the Hareem of the Pasha of
Egypt naturally directs the attention of the
reader to this remarkable man, who has for so
many years presided over the destinies of that
country. We hope that the following brief account of his career, with an abridgment of Mr.
Lane's account of " The Government " of Egypt,
may fitly conclude this volume.]

ACCOUNT OF MOHAMMAD 'ALEE, AND THE GOVERNMENT OF EGYPT.

Mohammad 'Alee, or Mehemet Ali, was born in 1769, at
Kavalla, a town of Roumelia, on the northern shore of the
Grecian Archipelago. His father, Ibrahim Aga, was head of
the police of the district of Kavalla. Mohammad 'Alee
having entered into business as a dealer in tobacco, was successful in trade, and increased his prosperity by an advan-
tageous marriage. When the French invaded Egypt, and the
Sultan found it necessary to collect troops in the various provinces of his empire, Mohammed 'Alee came to Egypt as
second in command over three hundred men, which was the
military contingent furnished by Kavalla ; and he was
present at the battle of Aboukir in 1799. He soon distin-

guished himself by his intrepidity, promptitude, and sagacity, and was promoted to a rank which placed under his command one thousand men. By degrees he became the favoured chief not only of the Albanian soldiers employed in Egypt, but of the chiefs of the Mamelukes; and when Kourschid Pasha was deposed, in 1805, in the rebellion of which Cairo became the centre, Mohammad 'Alee was elected governor of Egypt in his place. The Sultan, aware of his rising power and ambitious character, appointed him Pasha of Jidda, but he continued in Egypt, and the Sultan sent a fleet to compel him to leave the country. By the interference however of the Captain Pasha and the French consul, he managed to retain his government in Egypt, and to regain, at least ostensibly, the favour of the Sultan. But the Sultan was not long satisfied; in 1806 he made another attempt to remove Mohammad 'Alee from Egypt by appointing him Pasha of Salonica. In this appointment he pretended to acquiesce, but did not enter upon his new government, in consequence, as he alleged, of the importunities of his soldiers, who would not allow him to depart from Egypt. The influence of his friends again prevailed, aided by the payment of a large sum of money, and he was again received into the Sultan's favour.

The Mamelukes, or Memlooks, were a military body who had been in effect the rulers of Egypt for more than four hundred years. They were instituted in the early part of the thirteenth century by Malek Salech, who purchased many thousands of slaves, with whom the markets of Asia were then abundantly supplied in consequence of the devastating wars of Ghengis Khan. He chose chiefly young men, natives of the Caucasian regions, whom he trained in military exercises, and embodied into a corps of 12,000 men. This corps, by its discipline and organization, soon became formidable to its masters, and its leaders became the rulers of Egypt till 1517, when the Sultan Selim I. marched into the country, defeated the Mamelukes near Heliopolis, took Cairo, and put to death Tomaun Bey, the last of the Circassian dynasty, which had ruled Egypt from 1382 till that time. Selim, however, was obliged to maintain the Mamelukes as a military aristocracy in Egypt. The Beys of the Mamelukes, of whom there were twenty-four, though subject to the Pasha of Egypt, continued to be the governors of twenty-four districts. The Beys were elected out of the body of Mamelukes, who, from their military superiority, maintained a power almost independent of the Sultan and the Pasha. On the 21st of July, 1798, when the French army approached the great Pyramids, they saw the whole Mameluke force prepared for action under Mourad and Ibrahim Beys. The Mamelukes formed a splendid cavalry of about 5000 men, besides Arab auxiliaries; but their infantry, composed chiefly of fellahs, was contemptible. The Mamelukes had no idea of the resistance of which squares of disciplined infantry are capable. They charged furiously, and for a moment disordered one of the French squares, but succeeded no further, having no guns to support them. The volleys of musketry and grape-shot made fearful havock among them; and after losing most of their men in desperate attempts to break the French ranks, the remains of this brilliant cavalry retreated towards Upper Egypt, except a few who crossed the Nile and marched towards Syria.

After the English and the Turks had reconquered Egypt in 1801, the Mamelukes regained a good deal of their former power, though the Sultan was at first disinclined to favour them. By degrees, however, as he began to fear the ambition of Mohammad 'Alee, who continued to extend and consolidate his power, he was disposed to restore them to their old authority as a countercheck to the influence of the

Pasha. In 1811 Mohammed 'Alee felt himself sufficiently safe to put in execution a project which he had formed for destroying the power of the Mamelukes at a blow. His plan was treacherous and ferocious, but it was completely successful. The ceremony of investing his second son Toosoon with the caftan, when about to proceed at the head of an expedition against the Wahabees of Mecca, was the occasion which he chose for the execution of his purpose. The investiture was to take place in the citadel of Cairo, where he pretended to have prepared a banquet, to which the principal Mamelukes were invited, and between 400 and 500 of them came. Count Forbin, in his ' Voyage dans le Levant,' gives the following description of the scene :—

" That audacious militia, the Mamelukes, which, since the time of Malek Shah, had made Egypt to feel their power, were nearly destroyed by Mohammed Ali. They had received orders to hold themselves in readiness to take part in a grand ceremony, which was to precede the departure of his son for Mecca. 'That day,' said an inhabitant of Cairo to me, 'the sun rose the colour of blood !' The Pasha looked dark and melancholy : but recollecting that he was to preside at one of the most brilliant fêtes of the Mussulmans, he assumed a smile which contrasted remarkably with his general appearance. He had addressed the Mamelukes as the ' Elder Sons of the Prophet;' and called upon them, by the peace which subsisted between them, to celebrate with him the departure of his son for the Holy Tomb.

" In the meantime a number of faithful Albanians were concealed upon the ramparts, the towers, and behind the walls of the citadel. The Mamelukes arrived with the utmost confidence, and the gates were closed upon them. The Pasha had placed himself on the summit of a terrace, seated on a carpet, smoking a magnificent *narguile* (Persian pipe), from whence he could see every motion without being seen; behind him were three of his confidential officers. He regarded the scene below with a fixed and terrible look, without speaking a word; the signal was given to fire, and the massacre of the Mamelukes commenced. They were adorned, or rather encumbered, with their finest arms, and mounted on noble horses; but their numbers, their courage —all were useless—they were destroyed!"

Such of the Mamelukes as escaped the indiscriminate massacre within the walls of the castle, were seized and beheaded; and numbers in the towns and villages, on the calamity which had befallen their brethren being made known, shared a like fate. The remnant retired to Dongola in Nubia; but they were scattered by Ibrahim Pasha, and from that period the total destruction, or, at least, the complete subjugation, of the once proud Mamelukes may be dated.

The Wahabees were a Mohammedan sect in Arabia, who derived their name from Abdu-l-Wahab, a reformer of the religion of Mohammed, who was born about the end of the seventeenth century. This religious sect gradually attained to such a degree of temporal and political power that the very existence of the Turkish empire was endangered by them. They conquered Mecca in 1803 and Medina in 1804. Pilgrimages were stopped. From 1803 to 1809 no great caravan ventured to cross Arabia. They overran Syria, and concluded an alliance with Yúsuf, the rebellious Pasha of Bagdad. At length Mohammad 'Alee, in 1809, began to make preparations against them. To save his army from marching round by the northern gulfs of the Red Sea, he ordered timber for a flotilla of twenty-eight vessels to be got ready at Boolak, the port of Cairo, whence it was carried by camels to Suez, where the ships were constructed.

After the destruction of the Mamelukes, Mohammad 'Alee prosecuted the war against the Wahabees with vigour and perseverance. His son Toosooa Bey was the commander of the flotilla, which sailed down the Red Sea and entered Arabia in 1811; in 1812 he was defeated by the Wahabees near Medina, but he took that town in the course of the year. This conquest was mainly due to the impetuous courage of Thomas Keith, a Scotchman, known by the name and title of Ibrahim Aga, who took the outworks of Medina by storm. Mecca was taken in 1813. In 1814 Sa'ud, the chief of the Wahabees, died, and was succeeded by his eldest son Abdullah. The death of Sa'ud was the forerunner of the ruin of the Wahabees. The Egyptians continued to add to their conquests till 1815, when peace was concluded on terms unfavourable to Abdullah. Hostilities however suddenly broke out again, and another expedition was fitted out, under the command of Ibrahim Pasha, the eldest son of Mohammad 'Alee, who entered Arabia with his army in 1816. The Wahabees made an obstinate resistance, but in 1818 they were compelled to retreat to Der'aiyeh, where Abdullah was besieged by Ibrahim. The siege was long, but was carried on by Ibrahim with admirable skill and perseverance till December, 1818, when Abdullah surrendered. He and several of his family were sent to Constantinople, when after having been paraded through the streets for three days, they were beheaded. The greater part of the territories conquered from the Wahabees fell under the authority of Mohammad 'Alee. The power of the Wahabees, though broken, was not exterminated, and they gave him considerable trouble afterwards.

The navigation of the Nile from Rosetta to Alexandria has been attended for many years with considerable difficulty and danger, from the constant deposit brought down from the countries of Sennaar, Dongola, &c., and left at its mouth, which has formed a bar, that, when the wind blows on shore, is peculiarly dangerous to heavy-laden vessels. To avoid this difficulty, Mohammad 'Alee in the year 1819, partly, it is said, at the suggestion of Mr. Briggs, and partly from having lost a valuable cargo himself at Rosetta, came to the determination of cutting a canal from Mahmoodeyeh, a part of the environs of Alexandria, to a village called Atfeh, on the banks of the Nile, a distance of about forty miles. For this purpose he appointed Ismaël Pasha director of the works, with various subordinate officers, at the same time issuing orders to the various sheikhs of the provinces of Sakarah, Shizeh, Mensourah, Sharkieh, Menouf, Bahyreh, and some others, to supply each a quota of fellahs (amounting in all to 300,000 men, women, and children), and to encamp them along the site of the intended canal. The Pasha, however, had totally neglected to furnish either a sufficient supply of provisions for this immense multitude, or the requisite implements for excavation; the consequences were, that as he had appointed several regiments of the Nizam (or modern troops) at various stations along the line to prevent any relaxation, they were compelled to scrape the mud and sand up with their hands, which was conveyed by the women and children in baskets, and thrown on either hand. Having frequently to dig below the level of the sea, and being totally destitute of pumps to keep the water in check, they were compelled to work up to their knees in mud, which brought on ague. This, combined with labour to which they were totally unaccustomed, an insufficiency of provisions (their daily food consisting of a little lentil broth, a small quantity of bread, and a few beans), ill-treatment, want of water and protection from the cold air at night, caused a great mortality among them, frequently as many as a hundred dying in a day. In the hurry and confusion attending such a scene, as they fell they were buried among the earth thrown up from the remaining excavations. When this canal was finished, which was effected in seven months, 30,000 fellow-creatures were found to have been destroyed in this most barbarous expenditure of human power.

At the termination at Atfieh a sluice is erected to admit the Nile during its rise, and being closed on its retiring, the water is preserved for the purposes of navigation and irrigation. Alexandria is also supplied with water from this canal. The average breadth of this canal is about 220 feet, and the depth perhaps about 7½ feet, very serpentine at the commencement at Mahmoodeyeh, but gradually improving as you proceed. The navigation on this canal is a great source of revenue to the Pasha, as each kanjah pays a toll both going and returning, the original outlay having been very inconsiderable.

Besides the Mahmoodeyeh canal, many other canals have been made by direction of Mohammad 'Alee. The canal of Tanta, in the Delta, is about thirty miles long and about four yards wide; it has four sluices at Vames, and preserves its water throughout the year. The canal of Bouhyeh, on the Damietta branch of the Nile, is about thirty-five miles long and four yards wide. The canal of Bahyreh, on the Rosetta branch of the Nile, is nearly sixty miles long, and about five yards wide. Smaller canals have been excavated to a very considerable extent.

These canals, except that of Mahmoodeyeh, which is principally for navigation, are used chiefly for irrigation, the water being raised from them mostly by water-wheels, of which there are more than 50,000 in Lower Egypt, and of these about 38,000 have been introduced under the direction of Mohammad 'Alee. Each water-wheel is worked for the most part by three oxen and two men, and they work, on an average, 180 days in the year. Wherever water can be thus applied, the productive powers of the soil seem to be almost incalculable.

The Greek war of independence began in 1820. In 1824 Mohammad 'Alee sent a powerful army and fleet to Greece, to assist the Sultan. Though the Greeks were unable to drive the Turks and Egyptians out of their country, they were determined not to submit; and the contest had already lasted seven years when the battle of Navarino may be said to have decided the independence of Greece. If that naval battle had not taken place, the waste of human life would probably have been continued for several years longer, and the war have been terminated only by the extermination and transportation of the Greek population, which had been carried into effect on a large scale in the Morea by Ibrahim Pasha.

The naval battle of Navarino took place on the 20th of October, 1827, between the French, English, and Russian combined fleet, on one side, and the Turco-Egyptian fleet, which was anchored in the Bay of Navarino, on the other side. The English had three ships of the line and four frigates, the French three ships of the line and two frigates, and the Russians four ships of the line and four frigates. The combined fleet of the Turks and Egyptians consisted of three ships of the line and twenty-five frigates, besides smaller vessels. Admiral Codrington had the command of the combined fleet, and his object was to oblige Ibrahim Pasha to evacuate the Morea. After some desultory negotiations and some evasions on the part of Ibrahim, the English admiral resolved to attack Ibrahim's fleet. The Turco-Egyptians were completely defeated, with the loss of their three ships of the line, four of their frigates, and about forty or fifty smaller vessels. A convention followed, by which Ibrahim undertook to evacuate the Morea, and to restore the Greek prisoners whom he had sent to Egypt to their native country. The Egyptian ships which had not been destroyed were restored to the Pasha of Egypt. The Sultan, however, still continued to assert his right of domination over Greece, and the emancipation of Greece was not established till March, 1829, when the Conference of London laid down the principle of their independence, and the successful campaign during the same year of the Russians against the Turks induced the Sultan to acknowledge it by an article of the treaty of Adrianople, September, 1829.

Mohammad 'Alee now busied himself in the improvement of his country and of his public establishments. Though the means which he employed are little in accordance with our notions of the manner in which a government should treat its subjects, it must be admitted that he executed in a short time a number of extraordinary works. His military and naval conscriptions, however, induced many of the inhabitants of Egypt to abandon their country, and take refuge in Syria, where they received the protection of Abdallah, pasha of Acre. This afforded Mohammad 'Alee a pretext for commencing a war in Syria, which country he had obviously formed the design of annexing to Egypt, and then raising his pashalik into an independent kingdom.

Having raised an army of 40,000 men, including eight regiments of cavalry, a large park of artillery, and a battering-train, he appointed his son Ibrahim Pasha commander-in-chief. A squadron of five sail of the line and several frigates was fitted out at the same time. Ibrahim invaded Syria, and took Gaza in October, 1831. In November the squadron set sail for Acre, and on the 9th of December he commenced the siege of that fortress. Little skill was displayed in conducting the operations either by land or sea, and after six months Acre was taken by storm, May 21, 1832. Abdallah Pasha, who conducted the defence with chivalrous courage, was sent prisoner to Egypt, where he was treated with the honour due to his bravery, and had a palace assigned for his residence on the island of Rhouda.

Meantime, the Sultan, who had in vain issued his firman commanding Ibrahim to withdraw his troops from Syria, declared war against him April 15, 1832. On the 13th of June in that year Ibrahim took Damascus. On the 7th of July he defeated the army of the Sultan at Homs, on the 1st of August took Aleppo, and on the 21st of December totally defeated and dispersed the Ottoman army at Koniah, in Anatolia, and took the Grand Vizier prisoner.

If Ibrahim had pushed on immediately for Constantinople, Mohammad 'Alee might possibly have been placed on the throne of the Sultan, but he did not leave Koniah till the 20th of January, 1833, and reached Kutayah on the 1st of February. Meantime the Sultan had applied to his old enemy Russia for assistance against his rebellious subject. The assistance was granted, and a Russian squadron and army had reached the Bosporus before Ibrahim had entered Kutayah. This determined Ibrahim to resort to negotiation, and by the treaty of Kutayah the Ottoman empire was saved from destruction. On the 6th of May, 1833, the Sultan, by a firman, confirmed Mohammad 'Alee in his government of Egypt, granting to him in addition that of Damascus, Tripoli, Said, Safed, Naplous, and Jerusalem, and on the 9th of May Ibrahim was ordered to repass the Taurus.

England and France now began to turn their attention to the transactions and the state of affairs in the East. An English agent and consul was permanently established at Alexandria, and other European powers followed the example.

Meantime Mohammad 'Alee continued to keep up his army and navy, sent officers to be instructed in ship-building in the English dock-yards, had a French officer of distinction to discipline his army, and a French Admiral at the head of his fleet. His government of Syria was exceedingly oppressive by heavy taxation and conscription, and insurrections began to break out in 1834, in the Haouran, and afterwards among the Druses and Naplousians. The Sultan, who had never ceased to form plans for the recovery of Syria from the power of Mohammad 'Alee, in 1834 began to raise troops in the eastern part of Asia Minor. Mohammad 'Alee at the same time was preparing to secure his independence. He fortified the passes of the Taurus, and built barracks at Antioch, St. Jean d'Acre, and other places. In 1838, Mohammed 'Alee announced to the consuls his intention before long to declare himself independent. But the Sultan had been preparing for him. After a series of indecisive movements, and many fruitless negotiations between both parties and the great European powers, the Sultan, in May, 1839, sent an army into Syria, which was supposed to amount to 80,000 men, with 170 guns. Ibrahim Pasha immediately assembled his army, which was said to consist of 55,000 infantry, 10,000 regular cavalry, 60,000 irregular cavalry, and 196 guns. The English and French governments, by their agents and by sending fleets to the coast of Syria, endeavoured to settle the differences between the contending parties, but in vain. On the 24th of June, 1839, Ibrahim Pasha attacked the Turkish army at Nezib, and so completely defeated it that the remains passed the frontier in complete disorder, leaving baggage, ammunition, and guns behind them. On the 4th of July the Turkish fleet deserted to Mohammad 'Alee. The Sultan Mahmoud died on the 30th June, and was succeeded by his son, Abdul Medjid, who was then only sixteen years of age, to whom, on the 16th of July, Mohammad 'Alee signified his determination to assert by force his right to the hereditary government of all the provinces then under his command, instead of that of Egypt only, which was offered to him by the new Sultan. The five allied powers, England, France, Austria, Prussia, and Russia, now interfered in a more peremptory manner, and negotiations ensued, which terminated in the withdrawal of France and the conclusion of a treaty between the remaining four powers and Turkey, to compel the submission of Mohammad 'Alee. The treaty was signed in London, July 15, 1840.

A fleet consisting of English, Austrian, and Turkish vessels immediately commenced operations to enforce the terms of the treaty. Beyrout, Acre, and Sidon were successively stormed and taken, and after much negotiation Mohammad 'Alee consented to relinquish Syria altogether, and the hereditary government of Egypt was bestowed upon him by the Sultan, January 11, 1841. The important political events of the life of Mohammad 'Alee here terminate.

He has three sons now living. Ibrahim Pasha was born at Kavalla in 1789. He is middle-sized, and very stout. His features are large, heavy, and marked by the small pox. Toosoon Pasha, the second son, died of the plague in 1813. Ishmail Pasha, the third son, was murdered by the blacks at Sennaar. Said Bey, the fourth son, was born in 1822. The fifth son is called Mohammad 'Alee.

Mohammad 'Alee is now 75 years of age. His bodily vigour is said to be breaking down, as might be expected, but his mental energy remains unimpaired. He is of the middle stature, stout, and robust; his features somewhat coarse, but very expressive, with dark grey eyes. Mr. St. John, who visited Egypt in 1832, has very minutely described his habits, both private and public, as they were at

L

that time. His dress was that of an ordinary Turkish gentleman. He slept little, rose before daybreak, left his hareem on horseback, and proceeded to his divan for the despatch of business, which usually occupied till about nine o'clock, at which hour consuls and other persons desiring a public audience generally arrived. In an hour or two they retired, and he repaired to his hareem, where he remained till about three or half-past three in the afternoon. But even here messages and notes were brought to him, and he attended to business. At half-past three he returned to the divan, and after giving audience, remained there, after taking a slight repast, diligently employing himself till ten or eleven o'clock at night. During this evening sitting he generally found time for a game or two at chess, a person, who seems to have been a sort of court buffoon, being in attendance to play with him.

The following is Mr. St. John's account of his general habits and manners :—

"Both the Pasha and his court are very plain at Alexandria ; but at Cairo, where, however, he spends but a small portion of the year, things are conducted with more state, though he is everywhere extremely accessible. Any person who has leisure, and knows no better mode of employing it, may go every evening to the palace, whether he have business there or not ; and if he does not choose to force himself upon the notice of the Pasha, he can enter into any of the other magnificent apartments, which are lighted up, as well as the audience chamber, and converse, if he pleases, with some of the numerous company there assembled. To show his Highness's close habits of business, it has been remarked to me, that when accidentally indisposed at Alexandria, and compelled to take exercise in his carriage instead of on horseback, he is known constantly to take out with him the public despatches. Driving to the banks of the canal, he has his

carpet spread upon the ground, and there, while coffee is preparing, he usually sits, reading and sealing his despatches.
He will then enjoy his coffee and pipe, and afterwards return
directly to the palace. This is one of his recreations. In the
hareem, he reads or has books read to him, or amuses himself
by conversing with the abler part of the eunuchs. At other
times he is employed in dictating his history; or in playing
at chess, to which, like most other Orientals, he appears to be
passionately addicted. In fact his active restless temper will
never suffer him to be unoccupied, and when not engaged
with graver and more important affairs, he descends even to
meddling. Nothing is too minute for him. For example, a
young Egyptian Turk, educated in the school of Cairo, now
professor of mathematics, and teacher of the young officers
at Alexandria, is compelled every week to give him an exact
account of the manner in which each of his pupils pursues
his studies. During the period in which he was pushing
forward the preparations necessary for putting his fleet to
sea, a much smaller portion of the day than usual was
devoted to his audiences and ordinary business. Indeed
he would frequently give audience in the arsenal, where
he spent a considerable part of his time; after which
he used to step into his little elegant state barge, and cause
himself to be rowed out into the harbour among his ships,
to observe the progress of the naval architects and ship-
wrights, and urge them forward by his presence; and in these
little excursions of business he was sometimes so deeply interested, that he would not return to the palace before twelve
o'clock; thus greatly abridging his hours of relaxation. The
accidents of the weather never interfere with his resolutions.
He will sometimes set out on a journey in the midst of a
heavy shower of rain or a storm, which has more than once
caused him very serious illness. His movements are sudden

and unexpected : he appears in Cairo or at Alexandria when least looked for, which maintains a certain degree of vigilance among the agents of government; though something of all this may perhaps be set down to caprice or affectation. In the gardens of Shoubra there is a small alcove, where the Pasha, during his brief visits to that palace, will frequently sit, about eleven or twelve o'clock at night, and, dismissing from about him all his courtiers and attendants, remain for an hour or two. From this alcove two long vistas, between cypress, orange, and citron trees, diverge and extend the whole length of the grounds; and in the calm bright nights of the East, by moon or star light, when the air is perfumed by the faint odours of the most delicate flowers, a more delicious or romantic station could hardly be found."—St. John's ' Egypt and Mahomad Ali,' Lond. 1834.

The substantial wealth of Egypt consists in its extraordinary power of agricultural production. In that country, wherever there is water there is fertility; and by irrigation, combined with even the rudest forms of cultivation, the desert itself may be subdued, and compelled to retreat. Much has been done, under the government of Mohammad 'Alee, to render the waste fruitful. The supply of water indeed, which depends on the inundations of the Nile, may be deficient, and other causes also may occasionally destroy the hopes of the husbandman, such as the hot winds of the desert, which sometimes dry up whole districts, even after irrigation, or a flight of locusts, which, darkening the atmosphere to a vast extent, descends in a dense mass on the fields of grain, and devours and destroys everything. Happily these checks to the fertility of Egypt are rare and partial. Mohammad 'Alee, however, has made many and vigorous attempts to render Egypt independent (as it is called) of other countries, by the introduction of manufactures. His efforts have been attended with little success; and the wisdom of his policy in this matter may well be doubted. Every hand in Egypt which is transferred from agricultural labour to the manufactures which have been artificially introduced into the country, is removed from a productive and profitable employment to one which has been exceedingly expensive, and, with few exceptions, unsuccessful and profitless. The loss, however, has fallen wholly on the treasury of the Pasha, and not on the consumers. Cotton manufactures, which are those chiefly produced in his factories, cost him more than the articles can be imported for, notwithstanding the low price of labour and the extreme cheapness of the raw material.

Mr. Lane has the following remarks on the changes which have been introduced into Egypt by Mohammad 'Alee.

" The exaggerated reports which have been spread in Europe respecting late innovations, and the general advance of civilization, in Egypt, induce me to add a few lines on these subjects. European customs have not yet begun to spread among the Egyptians themselves; but they probably will ere long; and, in the expectation that this will soon be the case, I have been most anxious to become well acquainted (before it be too late to make the attempt) with a state of society which has existed, and excited a high degree of interest, for many centuries, and which many persons have deemed almost immutable.

" The account which I have given of the present state of the government of this country shows how absurd is the assertion, that Egypt possesses a legislative assembly that can, with any degree of propriety, be called representative of the people. The will of the Pásha is almost absolute; but he has certainly effected a great reform, by the introduction of European military and naval tactics, the results of which have already been considerable, and will be yet more extensive, and, in most respects, desirable. Already it has removed a great portion of that weight of prejudice which has so long prevented the Turks from maintaining their relative rank among the nations of the civilized world: by convincing them that one of our branches of science and practice is so far superior to that to which they were accustomed, it has made them in general willing, if not desirous, to learn what more we are able to teach them. One of its effects already manifest might be regarded by an unreflecting mind as of no importance; but is considered by philosophical Muslim as awfully portentous, and hailed by the Christian as an omen of the brightest promise. The Turks have been led to imitate us in our luxuries: several of the more wealthy began by adopting the use of the knife and fork: the habit of openly drinking wine immediately followed; and has become common among a great number of the higher officers of the government. That a remarkable indifference to religion is indicated by this innovation is evident; and the principles of the dominant class will doubtless spread (though they have not yet done so) among the inferior members of the community. The former have begun to undermine the foundations of El-Islám: the latter as yet seem to look on with apathy, or at least with resignation to the decrees of Providence; but they will probably soon assist in the work; and the overthrow of the whole fabric may reasonably be expected to ensue at a period not very remote.

"The acquisition of a powerful empire, independent of the Porte, appears to have been the grand, and almost the sole, object of the present Pásha of Egypt. He has introduced many European sciences, arts, and manufactures; but all in furtherance of this project; for his new manufactures have impoverished his people. He has established a printing-office; but the works which have issued from it are almost solely intended for the instruction of his military, naval, and civil servants. A newspaper is printed at another press, in the Citadel : its paragraphs, however, are seldom on any other subject than the affairs of the government. It is in Turkish and Arabic. Sometimes, three numbers of it appear in a week : at other times, only one is published in a month.

"I have candidly stated my opinion, that the policy of Mohammad 'Alee is in several respects erroneous ; and that his people are severely oppressed : but the circumstances in which he has been placed offer large excuses for his severity. To judge of his character fairly, we should compare him with another Turkish reformer, his late nominal sovereign, the Sultán Mahmood. In every point of view he has shown his superiority to the latter; and especially in the discipline of his forces. While the Sultán was more closely imitating us in trivial matters (as for instance, in the new military dress which he introduced), Mohammad 'Alee aimed at, and attained, more important objects.* When we would estimate his character by the massacre of the Memlooks, a fact most painful to reflect upon, we should admit that he had recourse to this horrid expedient for a most desirable end."

* The dress worn by the military and some other officers of the Pásha of Egypt is still quite Turkish in every thing but the want of the turban, which is now worn by few of those persons, and only in winter ; the red cap alone, over which the muslin or Kashmeer shawl used always to be wound, being at present the regular head-dress. The trousers are very full from the waist to a little below the knee, overhanging a pair of tight leggings which form part of them. A tight vest (the sleeves of which are divided from the wrist nearly to the elbow, but generally buttoned at this part), a girdle, a jacket with hanging sleeves, socks, and a pair of red shoes, complete the outward dress generally worn ; but the jacket is sometimes made with sleeves like those of the vest above described, and the vest without sleeves ; and black European shoes are worn by some persons. The sword is now hung in our manner by a waist-belt. The dress of the private soldiers consists of a vest and trousers (the latter similar to those above described, but not so full), of a kind of coarse red serge, or, in summer, of white cotton, with the girdle, red cap, and red shoes.

The following account of the government of Egypt is abridged from Mr. Lane's 'Manners and Customs of the Modern Egyptians,' Lond. 1842.

Egypt has, of late years, experienced great political changes, and nearly ceased to be a province of the Turkish Empire. Its present Pásha (Mohammad 'Alee), having exterminated the Ghuzz, or Memlooks, who shared the government with his predecessors, has rendered himself almost an independent prince. He, however, professes allegiance to the Sultán, and remits the tribute, according to the former custom, to Constantinople : he is, moreover, under an obligation to respect the fundamental laws of the Kur-án and the Traditions; but he exercises a dominion otherwise unlimited. He may cause any one of his subjects to be put to death without the formality of a trial, or without assigning any cause : a simple horizontal motion of his hand is sufficient to imply the sentence of decapitation. But he is not prone to shed blood without any reason: severity is a characteristic of this prince, rather than wanton cruelty; and boundless ambition has prompted him to almost every action by which he has attracted either praise or censure.

In the Citadel of Cairo is a court of judicature, called 'ed-Deewán el-Khideewee,' where in the Pásha's absence presides his 'Kikhya,' or deputy. In cases which do not fall within the province of the Kádee, or which are sufficiently clear to be decided without referring them to the court of that officer, or to another council, the president of the Deewán el-Khideewee passes judgment. Numerous guard-houses have been established throughout the metropolis, at each of which is stationed a body of Nizám, or regular troops. Persons accused of thefts, assaults, &c., in Cairo, are given in charge to a soldier of the guard, who takes them to the chief guard-house, in the Mooskee, a street in that part of the town in which most of the Franks reside. The charges being here stated, and committed to writing, he conducts them to the 'Zábit,' or chief magistrate of the police of the metropolis. The Zábit, having heard the case, sends the accused for trial to the Deewán el-Khideewee.* When a person denies the offence with which he is charged, and there is not sufficient evidence to convict him, but some ground of suspicion, he is generally bastinaded, in order to induce him to confess; and then, if not before, when the crime is not of a nature that renders him obnoxious to a very heavy punishment, he, if guilty, admits it. A thief, after this discipline, generally confesses, "'The devil seduced me, and I took it.'" The punishment of the convicts is regulated by a system of arbitrary, but lenient and wise, policy: it usually consists in their being compelled to labour, for a scanty sustenance, in some of the public works; such as the removal of rubbish, digging canals, &c.; and sometimes the army is recruited with able-bodied young men convicted of petty offences. The Pásha is, however, very severe in punishing thefts, &c., committed against himself:—death is the usual penalty in such cases.

There are several inferior councils for conducting the affairs of different departments of the administration. The principal of these are the following.—1. The Council of Deliberation. The members of this and of the other similar councils are chosen by the Pásha, for their talents or other qualifications; and consequently his will and interest sway them in all their decisions. They are his instruments, and

---

* A very arbitrary power is often exercised in this and similar courts, and the proceedings are conducted with little decorum. Many Turkish officers, even of the highest rank, make use of language far too disgusting to be mentioned towards persons brought before them for judgment and towards those who appeal to them for justice.

compose a committee for presiding over the general government of the country, and the commercial and agricultural affairs of the Pásha. Petitions, &c., addressed to the Pásha, or to his Deewán, relating to private interests or the affairs of the government, are generally submitted to their consideration and judgment, unless they more properly come under the cognizance of other councils hereafter to be mentioned. 2. The Council of the Army. The province of this court is sufficiently shown by its name. 3. The Council of the Navy. 4. The Court of the Merchants. This court, the members of which are merchants of various countries and religions, was instituted in consequence of the laws of the Kur-án and the Sunneh being found not sufficiently explicit in some cases arising out of modern commercial transactions.

The ' Kádee ' (or chief judge) of Cairo presides in Egypt only a year, at the expiration of which term, a new Kádee having arrived from Constantinople, the former returns. He purchases his place privately of the government, which pays no particular regard to his qualifications; though he must be a man of some knowledge, an 'Osmanlee (that is, a Turk), and of the sect of the Hanafees. Few Kádees are very well acquainted with the Arabic language; nor is it necessary for them to have such knowledge. In Cairo, the Kádee has little or nothing to do but to confirm the sentence of his ' Náïb' (or deputy), who hears and decides the more ordinary cases, and whom he chooses from among the 'Ulama of Istambool, or the decision of the ' Muftee' (or chief doctor of the law) of his own sect, who constantly resides in Cairo, and gives judgment in all cases of difficulty. But in general, the Náïb is, at the best, but little conversant with the popular dialect of Egypt; therefore, in Cairo, where the chief proportion of the litigants at the tribunal of the

Kádee are Arabs, the judge must place the utmost confidence in the Chief Interpreter, whose place is permanent, and who is consequently well acquainted with all the customs of the court, particularly with the system of bribery; and this knowledge he is generally very ready to communicate to every new Kádee and Náïb. A man may be grossly ignorant of the law, and yet hold the office of Kádee of Cairo: several instances of this kind have occurred; but the Náïb must be a lawyer of learning and experience.

There are five minor courts of justice in Cairo; and likewise one at its principal port, Boolák; and one at its southern port, Masr El-'Ateekah. A deputy of the chief Kádee presides at each of them, and confirms their acts. The matters submitted to these minor tribunals are chiefly respecting the sales of property, and legacies, marriages, and divorces; for the Kádee marries female orphans under age who have no relations of age to act as their guardians; and wives often have recourse to law to compel their husbands to divorce them. In every country town there is also a Kádee, generally a native of the place, but never a Turk, who decides all cases, sometimes from his own knowledge of the law, but commonly on the authority of a Muftee. One Kádee generally serves for two or three or more villages.

Each of the four orthodox sects of the Muslims has its 'Sheykh,' or religious chief, who is chosen from among the most learned of the body, and resides in the metropolis; and these sheykhs, together with the Kádee, the Nakeeb el-Ashráf (the chief of the Shereefs, or descendants of the Prophet), and several other persons, constitute the 'Ulama (or learned men), by whom the Turkish Páshas and Memlook chiefs have often been kept in awe, and by whom their tyranny has frequently been restricted: but now this learned body

has lost almost all its influence over the government. Petty
disputes are often, by mutual consent of the parties at variance,
submitted to the judgment of one of the four Sheykhs first
mentioned, as they are the chief Muftees of their respective
sects; and the utmost deference is always paid to them.
Difficult and delicate causes, which concern the laws of the
Kur-án or the Traditions, are also frequently referred by
the Pásha to these Sheykhs; but their opinion is not always
followed by him.

The police of the metropolis is more under the direction
of the military than of the civil power. The chief of the
police is called the Zábit. His officers, who have no distinguishing mark to render them known as such, are inter-
persed through the metropolis: they often visit the coffee-
shops, and observe the conduct, and listen to the conversation,
of the citizens. Many of them are pardoned thieves. They
accompany the military guards in their nightly rounds
through the streets of the metropolis. Here, none but the
blind are allowed to go out at night later than about an
hour and a half after sunset, without a lantern or a light of
some kind. Few persons are seen in the streets later than
two or three hours after sunset. At the fifth or sixth hour,
one might pass through the whole length of the metropolis
and scarcely meet more than a dozen or twenty persons, excepting the watchmen and guards, and the porters at the
gates of the by-streets and quarters.

The markets of Cairo, and the weights and measures, are
under the inspection of an officer called the 'Mohtes'ib.'
He occasionally rides about the town, preceded by an officer
who carries a large pair of scales, and followed by the exe-
cutioners and numerous other servants. Passing by shops,
or through the markets, he orders each shopkeeper, one
after another, or sometimes only one here and there, to pro-

duce his scales, weights, and measures, and tries whether
they be correct. He also inquires the prices of provisions
at the shops where such articles are sold. Often, too, he
stops a servant, or other passenger, in the street, whom he
may chance to meet carrying any article of food that he has
just bought, and asks him for what sum, or at what weight,
he purchased it. When he finds that a shopkeeper has incorrect scales, weights, or measures, or that he has sold a
thing deficient in weight, or above the regular market-place,
he punishes him on the spot. The general punishment is
beating or flogging.

As the Mohtes'ib is the overseer of the public markets, so
there are officers who have a similar charge in superintending each branch of the Pásha's trade and manufactures; and
some of these persons have been known to perpetrate most
abominable acts of tyranny and cruelty.

Every quarter in the metropolis has its sheykh, whose influence is exerted to maintain order, to settle any trifling
disputes among the inhabitants, and to expel those who dis-
turb the peace of their neighbours. The whole of the metropolis is also divided into eight districts, over each of which
is a sheykh.

The members of various trades and manufactures in the
metropolis and other large towns have also their respective
sheykhs, to whom all disputes respecting matters connected
with those trades or crafts are submitted for arbitration; and
whose sanction is required for the admission of new members.

The servants in the metropolis are likewise under the
authority of particular sheykhs. Any person in want of a
servant may procure one by applying to one of these officers,
who, for a small fee (two or three piastres), becomes respon-
sible for the conduct of the man whom he recommends.
Should a servant so engaged rob his master, the latter gives

information to the sheykh, who, whether he can recover the stolen property or not, must indemnify the master.

The Coptic Patriarch, who is the head of his church, judges petty causes among his people in the metropolis; and the inferior clergy do the same in other places; but an appeal may be made to the Kádee. A Muslim aggrieved by a Copt may demand justice from the Patriarch or the Kádee; a Copt who seeks redress from a Muslim must apply to the Kádee. The Jews are similarly circumstanced. The Franks or Europeans in general, are not answerable to any other authority than that of their respective consuls, excepting when they are aggressors against a Muslim: they are then surrendered to the Turkish authorities, who, on the other hand, render justice to the Frank who is aggrieved by a Muslim.

The inhabitants of the country towns and villages are under the government of Turkish officers and of their own countrymen. The whole of Egypt is divided into several large provinces, each of which is governed by an 'Osmanlee (or a Turk); and these provinces are subdivided into districts, which are governed by native officers. Every village, as well as town, has also its Sheykh, who is one of the native Muslim inhabitants.

The revenue of the Pásha of Egypt is generally said to amount to about three millions of pounds sterling. Nearly half arises from the direct taxes on land, and from indirect exactions from the felláhs: the remainder principally from the custom-taxes, the tax on palm-trees, a kind of income-tax, and the sale of various productions of the land; by which sale, the government, in most instances, obtains a profit of more than fifty per cent.

The present Pásha has increased his revenue to this amount by most oppressive measures. He has dispossessed of their lands almost all the private proprietors throughout Egypt, allotting to each, as a partial compensation, a pension for life, proportioned to the extent and quality of the land which belonged to him. The farmer has, therefore, nothing to leave to his children but his hut, and perhaps a few cattle and some small savings.

The direct taxes on land are proportioned to the natural advantages of the soil. Their average amount is about 8s. per feddán, which is somewhat less than an English acre. But the cultivator can never calculate exactly the full amount of what the government will require of him. The felláh, to supply the bare necessaries of life, is often obliged to steal, and convey secretly to his hut, as much as he can of the produce of his land. He may either himself supply the seed for his land, or obtain it as a loan from the government: but in the latter case he seldom obtains a sufficient quantity; a considerable portion being generally stolen by the persons through whose hands it passes before he receives it. The oppressions which the peasantry of Egypt endure from the dishonesty of the Ma-moors and inferior officers are indescribable. It would be scarcely possible for them to suffer more, and live.

The Pásha has not only taken possession of the lands of the private proprietors, but he has also thrown into his treasury a considerable proportion of the incomes of religious and charitable institutions, deeming their accumulated wealth superfluous. The *household* property of the mosques and other public institutions the Pásha has hitherto left inviolate.

The tax upon the palm-trees has been calculated to amount to about a hundred thousand pounds sterling.

The income-tax is generally a twelfth or more of a man's annual income or salary, when that can be ascertained. The maximum, however, is fixed at five hundred piastres. In the large towns it is levied upon individuals; in the villages, upon houses. The income-tax of all the inhabitants of the metropolis amounts to eight thousand purses, or about forty thousand pounds sterling.

The inhabitants of the metropolis and of other large towns pay a heavy tax on grain, &c.*

* It remains to be added that great changes are now being made in various departments. Most of the evils of which the people of Egypt have hitherto had to complain have arisen from the vast expense incurred in war, from the conscription, and from the dishonesty of almost all the Pásha's civil officers.

THE END.